Keepers of the Flame

Reflections on the Holocaust, Israel and other Jewish themes.

Michael Yanuck MD PhD

For Jim Szana,
the best dentist I ever knew,
who served the native peoples of the Northern Plains
and eased my mind during difficult dental procedures
by telling me his sojourns to Holocaust memorials
as he worked on me.

My father,
who always gave generously to charitable causes,
especially those preserving the memory of the Holocaust.

And for Dvora Caspi – my mother-in-law,
a child of Holocaust survivors,
she marched on Washington with Martin Luther King.
She always came to the aid of persecuted peoples,
and more than anyone I ever knew
she was forever working to keep the flame alive.

FOREWORD

As a result of our lives being overtaxed and busy, my wife and I forgot all about lighting the Hanukkah candles this year.

Looking at our unused menorah, I remembered something someone in Tennessee told me: "If you're standing with one foot in the past and the other in the future, then you're pissing away the present."

Yes, I thought, nodding. Such was what I'd done.

"Then let's do it on our own schedule," my wife said. "We'll light the candles now..."

So, we placed the candles in the menorah and lit them. In turn, we were amazed at how long they stayed lit.

"They're still going," my wife said. "It's like the flame goes out and then it comes back again."

"Looking at the candles in the menorah," she continued, "it's reminding me of your family's traditional job in the temple.

According to family lore, my ancestors were the keepers of the flame within the Great Temple in Jerusalem.

"And you and your job," she added. "I was thinking about how you as a doctor, you are there to nourish that little bit of flame and get it to go stronger and more secure for as long as possible in every person and every body. Physical body. And how your ancestors' job was to keep that flame going, and you're still doing that – You're keeping the flame going."

Then, she turned.

"It sounds like the title of a book," she said. "Keepers of the Flame..."

Let us celebrate and share in the miracle that we have this breath of life, this human spirit, which is but one of many of God's Candles, miracles, shining in the world around us.
~~Rabbi Evon, Hanukkah Message

The process of writing... is the struggle against the art of forgetting, a struggle that is as much a part of life as melancholy is of death, a struggle consisting in the constant transfer of recollection into written signs...
--Peter Weiss, German dramatist and writer, 1916-1982.

CHAPTER ONE

The Last Night of Ballyhoo

While looking in on a patient at the nursing home, my girlfriend, Cathy, called from the auditions for 'The Last Night of Ballyhoo,' and asked if I wanted to audition for a role.

I told her, no, saying I couldn't imagine I'd fit.

"Mike, do you know what this play is about?" she asked.

"It sounds southern," I responded. "Like 'Driving Miss Daisy.'"

"No," she replied. "It's about a family of assimilated southern Jews who come to terms with their Jewishness."

"What?!" I responded. "I'll be right there."

As I drove along the West Tennessee country roads to the auditions, I thought about my Jewishness.

Being Jewish forces you to come to terms with alienation and man's inhumanity to man. Indeed, 'The Last Night of Ballyhoo' is set in the backdrop of the very focal point of the Jewish experience - The Holocaust.

I was six years old when I learned about the Holocaust: A new family had moved into the neighborhood. They had two boys who were about the same age as my brother and me. They were handsome and athletic, but somehow they didn't seem as carefree as the rest of us. It just seemed like they and their family were nervous and worried about something, as though some dark cloud constantly hovered over them.

Then, one day, I saw the older boy pacing back and forth on the street, repeating, 'I hate Hitler. I hate Hitler...' Returning home, I asked my mom, 'Who's Hitler?' She explained our new neighbors were 'Jewish', and Hitler was the leader in a place called 'Germany' of

1

a group called 'Nazis', who rounded up 'Jews', packed them in 'cattle cars', and shipped them away to places called 'concentration camps' where they were summarily lined up, instructed to take their clothes off and led into 'showers.' But they weren't really showers; instead, they were 'gas chambers', where the people were 'gassed' until dead. Afterwards, their bodies were burned in 'ovens', their ashes spewing into the sky from 'giant chimneys', creating dark clouds of smoke.

Listening in horror to these descriptions, I was overcome with sympathy and compassion for this new boy and his family.

No wonder they lived as though under a cloud, I thought.

And I experienced a deep sense of purpose, too: I told myself (that moment) that I would dedicate my life to see that nothing like that ever again happened to Jews or anyone.

Then, my mother added something that left me stunned; she said we were Jewish, too. Before that, I'd no awareness of my ethnicity and thought that we were just like everybody else.

In that split second I went from being another 'sunny Californian' to a forlorn Jew (I could literally feel myself peering apprehensively over my shoulder) like that dark cloud settled over me.

From that day forward, my life would never be the same...

As my awareness of my identity grew, I came to think that Jews were a fairly discernible minority. Then, I went to medical school in Houston and found - to my surprise - that the Jews there seemed to blend perfectly with everybody else.

I had no idea who was Jewish. People would ask me about temple and Israel and I wouldn't know why? Until later, when I learned later that it was because they were Jewish.

This was at times difficult to adapt to: Once, a professor invited me to attend his reformed temple. Midway through the service, I realized that I wasn't wearing a yamulke (skull cap) and put my hand over my head in respect to God, so as not to come before Him with my bare head. Behind me the people groaned.

"Who is this guy?" they said...

Now, I was living in the South again, having followed Cathy and her five children to a small town in Tennessee. Not long after arriving, I was invited to write for the local paper.

What follows are articles I wrote on the subject of the Holocaust, Israel and other Jewish themes. The good people of Paris permitted me to 'Wax Philosophical' on these topics (This being the title the editor of the Paris Post-Intelligencer chose for my column). The best compliment I ever received came from a patient who'd been a World War II veteran and told me, "Reading your articles, you have the feeling that this physician is bearing his soul."

So do I now bear my soul to you.

On this – My reflections on the triumphs and travails of my people...

.

CHAPTER TWO

'War' series renews my deep gratitude
Michael Yanuck
The Post Box
The Paris Post-Intelligencer, Paris, Tenn., Page 2, October 4, 2007

At the clinic I had the privilege of caring for many World War II veterans. When Tim Burns' came out with his "The War" series, I offered this piece.

Last week I was with my father visiting the fabulous natural wonders of Zion and Bryce National Parks in southwest Utah.

Although I enjoyed the time with my father, it was hard to be away. PBS was airing Ken Burn's documentary series, The War, and I wanted to be able to share the experience with the World War II vets who I serve at the VA clinic in Dover.

I came back to the clinic today, and talked to one of them. I asked if he'd been watching the series. He said that he didn't know anything about it.

I told him that I was anxious to watch tonight's broadcast because it dealt with The Battle of the Bulge. He said that he'd fought there.

I talked about the series, and its disclosure of the tragic losses in the Normandy landing at Omaha beach. He said that he'd fought there, too. He went on, saying that he had four brothers, and all of them fought in the war as well.

He shared a few stories, and then stopped. His eyes welled up, and he said that now he'd probably told me more about his experience than he'd shared with any of the members of his family...

Growing up Jewish, my awakenings to World War II came from a different perspective. I was exposed to survivors of Hitler's concentration camps.

One person in particular was my friend, Randy's, father. He had an odd habit of going into the shed behind the house every Sunday with a bushel of apples, and locking the door behind him.

One day, Randy followed him, and looked inside. He said that his father opened the bushel of apples, and dug into them like a man who was starving; ravenously devouring them like a crazed animal, who'd been without food for an interminable period time.

Randy's family was middle class, and, in every respect, enjoyed an abundance of material comforts. Nevertheless, Randy's father repeated this ritual every week of Randy's upbringing.

Talking to another World War II veteran, I asked him what his thoughts were on the war at the time that he was fighting it. He hesitated and reflected for a moment, then said, "Well, the way I saw it, the world had a problem, and it was our job to fix it."

I have no illusions about what the war means to me. Had it not been for the sacrifices of the brave men and women of this country who fought that war, I would not be here, nor would any of the members of the Jewish race.

I feel a deep sense of gratitude, and desire to uphold the principles that the veterans of World War II fought for.

When I serve my World War II veterans, it is with full recognition that these are the individuals who saved the world, and to whom I owe my very existence.

CHAPTER THREE

My friend's father fought for Adolf Hitler
Michael Yanuck
Waxing Philosophical
The Paris Post-Intelligencer, Paris, Tenn., Page 2, January 29, 2008.

I had been feeling as though I was straying too far from the town in my submissions, and was looking for something that would bring the focus back to Paris.

Then, this chance meeting with my kind-hearted friend, Mr. Dan Patterson, a town fixture in the community as Parks Activity director (and everyone's favorite Santa during the holidays) provided me with just such an opportunity...

At the girl's basketball game at Atkins-Porter, Mr. Dan Patterson pulled me aside. I'd been thinking about him; recently, I'd watched a re-run of "The Natural," and was reminded of the story that he had told me about his father, who'd been offered a contract to play professional baseball, but suffered an arm injury just before the season.

"Really," he said. "'Cause I saw a movie that made me think about you!"

In the past Mr. Patterson had inquired where my "people" came from. I had told him that my father's family had come from a stehtl (Jewish village) in Russia that no longer existed. Recently, he'd seen a film that drew on a character whose circumstances were not unlike my own.

"It was about a young Jewish American who goes to Russia after the fall of the Berlin Wall, looking for the village where his family came from," he said. "He employs two men - a German and his father - to help him find the village, and the three of them become great friends."

"But, as they get closer to the village, the German's father keeps having flashbacks," he continued. "In the end, you find out that during the war the father had actually been the Nazi SS officer who had ordered the burning of the town, and the murder of all its inhabitants..."

This, in turn, reminded me of a story.

While studying at the Weizmann Institute in Israel I had cultivated a close friendship with a German physics student named Georg (pronounced "Yorg"). After the summer, Georg went back to Germany, and I made plans to visit him there before returning to the States. There, he introduced me to his family.

Then, something odd happened. I was alone in my room, when Georg's father knocked on the door, and stumbled in. After an awkward silence, he spoke.

"I was a soldier in the war," he said. "It wasn't that I supported the government. I was simply drafted into the army."

Georg's family had planned a reunion in Denmark, and I was invited to come along and travel with them through Germany.

I looked forward to the journey. In particular, I was hoping to visit some of the concentration camps where my people perished.

But, on the way, Georg's father began experiencing crippling headaches. At times, he was so incapacitated that he couldn't arise from bed.

Georg informed me that his father was having a difficult time with his conscience, and my being Jewish had rekindled memories about the war.

As a result, I passed on the death camps, and, instead, sampled apple beer at Lake Constance, took in the beauty and lushness of Bavaria, and hiked the woods of the Black Forest.

Even in Denmark, there were reminders of the German occupation, with bunkers strewn all along the coast. Georg's father still seemed unsteady, and I was glad when we left the beach, and went touring the Legoland Amusement Park in Billund.

Georg had a deep social conscience. While in Germany, he alerted me to the plight of the Kurds.

Later, in Washington D.C., when I became active in the Kurdish struggle against the genocidal acts perpetrated by Saddam Hussein (who gassed the Kurds in Halabja), I worked with a number of committed German friends.

So, yes, my friend's father fought for Hitler's Third Reich. You never know from where the seeds of humanity will spring.

Postscript: Years later, I would share this story at the screening of a film about a Jewish American couple who went to Oppenheim, Germany to live, and were the first Jews to re-enter that community since the Holocaust. This was a difficult time when I was becoming more and more discouraged about writing. Nevertheless, friends supported me through this period, like Natan, a survivor of a form of cancer that was thought to be fatal, who, in response to my sharing of this story, wrote as follows:

"Dearest Michael, Your English is wonderful and very profound. Your words comes out like a story. I know that being married puts some limitations, without having an extra space. Trying to find a position which will suit you as a doctor will temporary block and put some stress in your ability and desire to write - but believe me, Mr. Yanuck, everything in your life will come to its own place like a puzzle, and you'll be able to pursue your wishes and dreams. I know you so little, but something about you makes me feel close to you. I think you are a great and special person, with high levels of modesty which you're hiding behind. Such a wonderful quality will help you in a long run. I am certain that one day you will not only be successful as a physician, but also as a great story teller (thanks to the love and passion to write which you were born with).
I want to be there to say "I told you so"!!! Much love - Natan."

More about Natan in later.

CHAPTER FOUR

The day I just wept and wept
Michael Yanuck
Waxing Philosophical
The Paris Post-Intelligencer, Paris, Tenn., Page 2, February 7, 2008.

The Democratic Primaries were coming to Tennessee, sparking considerable debate, particularly over the candidacy of Senator Barack Obama, who provided the inspiration for this piece...

I have an older friend who comes from this area. He carries himself with a certain dignity, and I think a lot of his opinions, and his penchant for moral authority.

But, the other night, he thoroughly surprised me, when, in the midst of a discussion about the Presidential candidates, he said that he was going to vote for "Obama."

"Really?" I said.

"Oh, yeah," he responded. "That Hilliary and her husband made up my mind ... in South Carolina. When they pulled out the race card, well, that was the last straw."

I didn't expect this of my friend. After all, he'd grown up in the segregated South.

Then, I remembered another time when I wasn't expecting something.

It happened while I was living in Washington, D.C. The Holocaust Museum had just opened to a lot of fanfare, and a cousin, who volunteered at the museum, offered me tickets to the initial screening.

I wasn't interested, though. I thought, What did the Jewish Holocaust have to do with the United States?

But my brother was visiting, and wanted to go.

I was worried because he had a tendency to get emotional over that sort of thing, and decided to accompany him.

At the museum we walked past displays that addressed the Nuremberg Laws, and Krystalnacht (The Night of Broken Glass), and then the concentration camps, and I watched my brother for signs that he might break down.

For myself, I'd seen it all before. I thought that the exhibits were artistic, but nothing new. I appreciated the work that went into assembling the collections of albums and pictures of those who had perished, but didn't feel particularly moved.

Then, we arrived at the lowest level of the museum, and I was confronted by something that I wasn't prepared for. This level was devoted to those people (mostly Germans) who had risked their lives to protect persecuted Jews.

I looked out, confused.

This isn't right, I thought. The Jews were hated, and they were murdered. What were these people doing?

And then, it hit me - there were people who cared.

And I moved away from my brother, and sought a place in the shadows where I could be alone, and unseen.

And I wept, and wept, and wept.

Since a child, when I'd first learned about the Holocaust, I had put myself there, and imagined what it would have been to watch my family lined up, and then marched into the gas chambers. What it might have been to be in a concentration camp myself.

I'd not only forgotten that humane feeling existed - I didn't believe it.

And, yet, it turned out that there were those who had put their well-being (indeed, their very lives) in jeopardy to help others.

And I wept for hope, and the possibility of friendship, and a better world that I might believe in.

"I think it's about time that we look beyond race," my friend said, "and see people for who they are and what they stand for, and not judge them based of the color of their skin...."

Postscript: Among the responses that I received for this article included the following: "Very nice....I went to the Hol. Museum in Israel last February and it was astonishing. I cried like a baby at the end...."

CHAPTER FIVE

Hitler, my country, and Will Strickland
Michael Yanuck
Waxing Philosophical
The Paris Post-Intelligencer, Paris, Tenn., Page 2, March 24, 2008.

Before submitting this piece, I met with my editor, and expressed concerns that I'd overdone stories about World War II veterans, and perhaps I should shelve this one.

He responded by saying that there were some subjects that could never be written about enough, and this was one of them.

Recently, I received a letter from the family of Mr. Will Strickland, a World War II veteran who I had cared for. In it they wrote: "In October 2007 you wrote a beautiful and heartfelt letter published in the Paris [Post] Intelligencer ['War' series renews my deep gratitude, October 4, 2007]. Will and I were so grateful and impressed with the letter. Will has a copy by his bed at Henry County Healthcare. He tells me he reads it often because of your understanding of the experience of veterans..."

Truth-be-told, I haven't the slightest inkling of what veterans went through. All I know is that if it weren't for men like Will Strickland, I wouldn't be here.

Here's one more piece meant to reflect what WWII veterans mean to me.

Recently, a woman asked about my religion, and when I'd become aware of my faith.

It happened when I was perhaps six or seven years old. There'd been a new family that had recently moved into my neighborhood. The family's two boys were about my age, but, despite being handsome and athletic, they seemed somehow different from my other friends, as though a dark cloud hung over them.

One day this family's older boy was trudging about in the bright California sunshine, and I heard him proclaim, "I hate Hitler."

Returning home, I asked my mother who Hitler was? She explained that our new neighbors were Jewish, and Hitler was a leader in Germany who had ordered the mass extermination of Jews.

She described how the Jews had been sent to something called "concentration camps," then put into "showers" in which they were "gassed," before finally transferred into "furnaces" in which their remains were burned, with great billows of smoke and ash rising from huge chimneys, and spilling into an ever darkening sky.

Listening to my mother, my heart went out to this neighborhood boy, and I felt as though I could understand why his family seemed more reserved than the rest of us.

And I wanted to fight people like Hitler and all those who would oppress people like the Jews (or any race), so that they wouldn't have to live under tyranny.

But the story didn't end there, as my mother had something else to tell me. She said that we, too, were Jews. Prior to this, I'd had no knowledge my separate identity, and thought that we were just like everyone else.

So, I suppose that I might have preferred to simply been an American, with a tradition of fighting for freedom, as well as coming to the aid of others who'd been persecuted.

But the story didn't end there, as my mother had something else to tell me. She said that we, too, were Jews. Prior to this, I'd had no knowledge my separate identity, and thought that we were just like everyone else.

So, I suppose that I might have preferred to simply been an American, with a tradition of fighting for freedom, as well as coming to the aid of others who'd been persecuted.

But, as it turned out, I owe my country more than my appreciation, as I am also in its debt for saving my race...

Unfortunately, this story doesn't end here, either. The day after I received the letter from Mr. Strickland's family, I called over to the nursing home intent on paying him a visit. I wanted to sit and chat about his time in the service, and ask him my own questions about following my conscience.

So the reply that I received was unexpected. "He's no longer with us, Dr. Yanuck," the nurse said. "He passed away earlier in the week..."

Not long ago, Mr. Strickland had been sharing stories with me, like the time that he was insulted by matinee idol, Errol Flynn.

"He told me that since I was a lowly stagehand, I should keep my mouth shut whenever he walked by," Strickland had said. "I let him have it then."

At the time he'd been recovering from a heart attack. "Getting old is not for wimps," he'd told me.

On the contrary, growing older requires intense courage - and he'd had that kind of courage, as well as humor, and goodwill.

Talking to his family, they were kind, and asked me to accept a small library of books that belonged to Strickland.

"Most of these books cover battles in which he, family and classmates were personally involved the world over," his sister reiterated. "Some have short written comments. Will was so anxious they go to you because you have a rare understanding of the horrors of war..."

Walking to the McEvoy Funeral Home, I felt sad.

Another voice from our "greatest" generation was gone, I thought. Now, I'm left alone to answer my questions.

Perhaps, it's fitting, though, that I should ponder the issues of my day on my own. Mr. Strickland rose to the call of his generation. Now, it's time for me to rise to mine.

I just hope that I can do justice to his example.

CHAPTER SIX

Allow me to respond to bigotry.
Michael Yanuck
Waxing Philosophical
The Paris Post-Intelligencer, Paris, Tenn., Page 2, December 26,
2008.

*Even my editor was squeamish about including much of the contents
of the letter that I received, and only permitted a small portion of it in
print.*

My "Imam" piece garnered some attention.
One reader wrote a letter that was rather long and convoluted, so
I'll address it in parts. Here are a few excerpts:
"Yanuck, I am still wondering why Jews identify with blacks,
etc? ... Why, for many, many centuries even before Christ, have Jews
been despised, ostracized and even hated by peoples wherever they
lived? ... Trouble makers? I suspect, considering my experiences
with Jews in New Orleans....
"Then, in the 1930s-40s, (Jews in) Europe allowed (them)selves
to be gathered like cattle to camps to be slaughtered .... But, for
nearly six decades since, like yapping dogs behind a screened-door,
have whined about and accused others for allowing Jews to be
abused or killed off, even though d--- few of the Jews raised arms to
prevent their own families from being slaughtered. ..."
I can't begin to imagine what the victims of the Holocaust
experienced, and it saddens me when blame is issued against the
victims of atrocities.

In general, I regard the demise of my departed European brethren as little different from that of Jesus, and wonder if the reader holds Jesus with the same contempt that he expresses for Jews?

As for the reader's assertion that family members of those trapped in Hitler's Europe did little, whereas I can't speak for all, permit me to describe the efforts of a friend's grandmother, who is now 96 years old.

After leaving Czechoslovakia just before the Nazis took control, she labored tirelessly for years to help her family do the same.

When she could not acquire passports for them to enter the United States, she arranged visas to Cuba. She wrote her family countless letters; however, unbeknownst to her, the Red Cross was withholding her family's replies for fear that the contents of their letters would stir panic.

Finally, the Red Cross released those letters. They documented the daily, grinding, dehumanizing events suffered by her family members all the way to their ultimate demise in the concentration camps. To this day, the grandmother mourns for them still.

As for the reader's experiences in New Orleans, I do not know what happened to him there; I can only imagine that the horrors he lived through are only rivaled by those of the gas chamber, so as to justify such unguarded expressions of condemnation for an entire race.

And concerning the tendency of "Jews to identify with blacks, etc," speaking for myself, whenever someone is willing to look beyond my "differences," and bless me with the greatest gift - that being, friendship - I realize that there is nothing more valuable, and wish to extend it to others.

Postscript:

I was actually surprised that my editor printed this submission; given that he regarded the reader's letter as "filth,"it didn't seem that he particularly felt as though it merited a response.

Nevertheless, a number of readers appreciated the article, and among the responses that I received was the following: "Dr. Yanuck, Your reply in the recent edition of the PI was awesome! Hopefully, it will make those wrapped in hate of anyone who looks or thinks differently from them ashamed of their provincial responses. Hopefully, your letter will inspire some of the locals to reflect on their own values and realize how full of pus they really are!... Keep up the good work... Don."

CHAPTER SEVEN

Letter from the Holocaust.
Michael Yanuck
Waxing Philosophical
The Paris Post-Intelligencer, Paris, Tenn., Page 2, March 6, 2009.

I'd been sitting on this story since New Year's, feeling that I'd already written too much about the Holocaust, and should abandon the subject.

But after reading William Barr's attack on Muslim immigrants Feb. 19, I decided that accounts like the following still have a place, and offer a glimpse at what public attacks on a particular group can, as Barr would say, "morph into."

On a cold winter night in New England, my friend and I were snowed in while visiting her grandmother. At 96 years old, the grandmother is frail and infirm, and attended to by a caretaker named Lisa, who kindly arranged a room for my friend and me to sleep.

"It's hard to make a lot of space," Lisa said, "because Marietta [the grandmother] keeps everything. She has gas bills from 1973. Me, I pay the bill, and after three months, I throw it away.

"She has things that are a hundred years old. You think I'm kidding? Look over here. In this box, there's a passport from when Marietta came over here from Czechoslovakia in the 1930s. Here's something that Marietta wrote about her mother. Look at this."

The note read, "I want to write about my mother, but I am finding it much more difficult. I am not sure why. Maybe because I feel guilty.

"I think I gave her a very hard time, especially during my adolescence. At that time, I was an intellectual snob and I looked down on anyone who was not interested in my intellectual topics."

Gazing up from the note, I looked in the direction of the grandmother, and tried to imagine her as this precocious little girl.

"My mother was a simple woman who had an eighth-grade education, as was the usual custom for girls at that time," the note continued. "She was loving and totally devoted to my father.

"My mother's name was Ida Schlosser. She was born in 1875 in Prague. I do not know much about my mother's early years. I think she was quite overwhelmed by her boisterous and somewhat undisciplined younger brothers.

"I think she was pretty as a young girl and she proudly told me that she had long blond hair and beautiful regular teeth.

"Her life was dominated by the prevailing tradition that a girl was expected to learn domestic arts and to wait for a suitable man to get married to. A 'suitable or acceptable' man was understood to be Jewish, already well established and preferably wealthy.

"When she was 16, my uncle Rudolph, was falling behind in his studies and my grandmother asked the director of the Jewish orphanage to recommend a tutor. Dr. Stern recommended a young law student, Fritz Eidlitz.

"Fritz came, and all the children fell in love with him. For my mother, it was love at first sight. She adored him from the minute she met him, and she knew that he was the man for her.

"But there was a big problem. He was not 'suitable and acceptable' in the traditional sense. He was Jewish, but he was a student, not yet well established and completely penniless."

The story ended there, as I could not find a subsequent page with its continuation.

Needless to say, Ida did go on to marry the penniless Fritz; the grandmother was their only child.

Sifting through more contents from the box, I came across a curious handwritten note.

"Can you go home again?" it read. "1933 Hitler elected. 1938 Austria. Sept. 1938 Munich - Chamberlain - 'peace in our time' - Sudetenland. Jan. 18, 1939, we left. March 15, 1939, Hitler in Prague."

Then, something labeled, "Letter from dad, Prague, October, 1941:

"We are happy about all your efforts for us. We got your

telegram about the visa to Cuba, but the Cuba delegation is in Berlin, Germany, and we would have to go there to get the visa.

"We have to finish our preparations in Prague to get the passports, and that will take still several weeks. The Jewish community will pay for our passage on the ship. So we do not have to worry about that expense.

"The second difficulty is to get the permission to leave, and that is more difficult to get. We will do what we can to get permission, and we will let you know by telegram. We thank you for the many efforts and we are happy to see you soon."

Finally, tucked away in a corner was a stack of papers that carried a more ominous subheading: "Letter from Gerta Schlosser, wife of my cousin, Gerd Schlosser, dated Oct. 10, 1945, answering my urgent requests for a report of what happened to all my relatives in the Holocaust. Gerta was the only one who survived."

That's when I knew that I had stumbled upon something of personal interest.

You see, in a previous column [Dec. 26, 2008] I had briefly described one woman's tireless efforts to get her family out of Czechoslovakia in the time of Hitler, only to learn that all had perished in the Holocaust.

Now, I was holding in my hands the very letter that had announced the end of her world.

To be continued...

Postscript: In response to this article, William Barr wrote the following:

"Michael Yanuck's silly attempt to stifle debate on "diversity" or immigration by injecting his Holocaust stories onto this page suggests that the American people may genocide Muslims if we do not welcome them. Just how many more ought the country to absorb, pray? All the ones with good character references, as Yanuck intimates? That would cover the 9-11 hijackers, whose visas required attestation of the same. If Yanuck wanted to write about the dispossession of hundreds of thousands of Muslims and Christians in his beloved Israel, he could shed light on an important issue. Don't hold your breath. When it comes to the national question, whether in Netanyahu/Lieberman Israel or in this country, that's just something Yanuck wants to sweep under the rug and leave outside the realm of public debate. [William W. Barr is the former headmaster of Cottage Grove School]"

A number of readers were incensed by Barr's comments; one of them wrote the following:

"Where he [Barr] accused you of trying to stifle debate and that Americans might consider genocide against Muslims, I wondered how in the world he could say that. My thoughts concerning your previous articles were that we should treat all people regardless of ethnicity/religion with dignity..."

My fiancee's mother (daughter to the grandmother in this story) was also taken aback by Barr's off-handed remarks.

"He has a nerve to say that your story isn't relevant," she said. "In the town in Czechoslovakia where my mother grew up and knew most of these people, they're having a Neo-Nazi March. It's being broadcasted on the news right now, as we speak..."

As for me, my initial response to Barr's comments was, "What does Israel and Netanyahu have to do with his attacks on Muslim immigrants in this country?"

Interestingly, Barr used the same language that I'd seen in some hate-mail; namely, the use of terms like "stifle debate" to justify expressions of bigotry.

As the time drew near for my next submission, I considered responding to Barr, citing previous articles that I'd written expressing my concern about the discrimination against Muslims in Israel, and re-stating my belief that there are fanatics of every religion - whether they be Muslim or Christian or Jewish - and, for all of us, it seems that the choice is the same: You can regard others with fear, or you can approach them with love; you can endeavor to hurt, or you can make efforts to heal.

In the end, however, I decided to forego further exchanges with Barr. Really, I'd been taught that, in the Jewish tradition, the worst offense that one could commit was to humiliate another in public, and I figured that I'd done enough of that, and, for anyone who looked, they could see Barr for who and what he was.

And I wanted to get back to the stories that mattered to me - about the people in my life (and patients I'd cared for) who had touched my heart.

CHAPTER EIGHT

Part II of letter from the Holocaust: The Terezin Ghetto
Michael Yanuck
Waxing Philosophical
The Paris Post-Intelligencer, Paris, Tenn., Page 2, March 13, 2009.

In a December submission, I had briefly described the tireless efforts of a friend's grandmother to get her family out of Czechoslovakia in the time of Hitler, only to learn that all had perished in the Holocaust. What follows is the fateful letter that bore that news:

"Dear Marietta, I have received today your second letter, and I am ashamed to have left you so long without an answer. The reason is that I was always a little afraid of writing to you of the dreadful things I have to tell you.

"In January 1942, Gerd [the grandmother's favorite cousin] and I [Gerta Schlosser, Gerd's wife and the writer of this letter] went to Terezin [a Jewish ghetto organized by the Nazis]. It was rather bad there in the beginning; we were in barracks, men and women separately.

"When Gerd wanted to see me, he had to carry trunks [to her barrack] when there was a new transport, or to push a coal wagon and unload the coal; then he would get an hour to be together with me.

"Or I had to go peeling potatoes in his barrack - stealing potatoes as well, for we got little food - or to go and scrub floors.

"It was not easy to get there anyhow, you needed "protection" and a lot of energy. Later on, Gerd got a ... permit, because he was working as an electrician, so he could see me more often. It was only after the evacuation of the Aryans from the town that we could circulate freely.

"I think that your parents [Fritz and Ida Schlosser] arrived in April 1942. Uncle Fritz [how the writer consistently refers to the grandmother's father] didn't feel too well because of his prostate, but was well looked after by Era Klapp, who didn't survive, but his old parents are alive.

"Your parents were rather 'lucky,' for they lived in the same house, side by side, in one room the women, in the other the men, so that they were together all day.

"Gerd was very often with them. Later, when we were allowed to walk in the town, we went there together. Uncle Fritz was always the same, joking and full of optimism.

"In spring 1942, came also Victor and Edie [the grandmother's uncle and aunt]; they stayed only two days in Terezin.

"Gerd tried everything to keep them there, but it was not possible. The whole transport, with a few exceptions, went to Poland. We were very upset, for it was only vanity on the part of one of the leaders that prevented their staying.

"Karl Fischer, who held a good position there, had tried his best. By the way, Karl, with his wife, returned and are living in Prague. Karl was very ill, an ulcer; his wife was ill, too, with the lungs.

"Gerd was never one day ill, yet you see, it was always the most improbable that happened.

"Victor and Edie were very courageous; I admired Edie. They were smiling and optimistic.

"A few months later came Herta with Emil and Hansi [all cousins to the grandmother]. The boy got scarlet fever and so they stayed there, else they would have gone immediately to Poland. Hansi was very proud that he 'protected' the family.

"You can imagine how disappointed Herta was when she found that her parents were not there. I grew very fond of Herta, for I saw that she was genuinely good; in Terezin, most people had altered or showed their real self - but Herta remained as she was.

"In July 1943 came Aunt Mathilde; she died there after a year. A few weeks later came Kokschi and Martha [uncle and aunt to the grandmother].

"Friedel [a young cousin] was in Lipa since 1940, I think; that was a farm where Jewish boys had to work. It was the greatest blow for the parents to be without Friedel.

"In spring 1943, there were many transports leaving Terezin, and your parents had to go, too - I am not sure about the date. Gerd tried to plead Uncle Fritz's illness, but nothing could be done.

21

"Herta and I packed for them, for Uncle Fritz was discussing politics and Aunt Ida was so flustered that she could not do anything. Uncle Fritz didn't lose his humor and, when Aunt Ida saw it, she became more courageous.

"There were always 'Transportbondes,' i.e., lies, and that time they said it was a very good transport that went to Silesia. We were glad it didn't go to Poland.

"We all were silly enough to believe all those things, the good political news, etc. Only Gerd never believed them - but then, he didn't believe the bad things either, and they were true.

"In summer 1943, it was Herta leaving, then came Friedel to Terezin to the joy of all of us. He had become a very handsome, broad-shouldered, tall boy, very intelligent, really a fine boy.

"So our family was together for a short time, but we knew it wouldn't be for long. In September 1943, there was a transport again, and Gerd's parents had to go. Twice already, we had succeeded to get them out of previous transports; but this time, nothing was to be done. So Friedel went with them voluntarily ...."

Just then, my friend, who had been reading the letter with me, gasped, and looked at me. "The grandson went with his grandparents to the death camps!" she said.

To be continued.

CHAPTER NINE

Part III, The letter from the Holocaust: The Death Camps
Michael Yanuck
Waxing Philosophical
The Paris Post-Intelligencer, Paris, Tenn., Page 2, March 20, 2009.

While snowed in at the home of a friend's grandmother, I came across a box of papers. Inside was a letter documenting the fate of her family in the Holocaust. This is the conclusion of that letter:

"Meanwhile, conditions in Terezin [a Nazi imposed Jewish ghetto] had improved considerably. 'It is too good to last,' Gerd [the grandmother's favorite cousin, and husband to the writer of this letter] said.

"In September 1944, they came with a new gigantic swindle. They said they needed working transports of young men, a new camp was supposed to be founded in Saxonia.

So when Gerd had to go, I didn't mind too much, for we thought the end was near, and I believed Gerd would be better off in Germany when the end came than in Terezin, where they could do to us what they liked.

"But Gerd must have had a premonition; he was terribly sad when he left me, worrying about me. All young women were very unhappy, so the Germans were so 'kind' to allow us 'to join our husbands.'

"I didn't go voluntarily; I knew that Gerd would be against it. But when I got the convocation, I was quite enthusiastic and left, though I could have stayed, as I was teaching the wife of the Jewish Alderman [mayor overseeing the ghetto].

"We went to Saxonia all right, but we went through it, traveled all day and all night, penned together like cattle, and arrived in Auschwitz.

"I must again ask your forgiveness. I had stopped because I was tired and lacked the courage to continue.

"Well, in Auschwitz, they told us to leave our luggage in the train and then came the famous 'selection' of which you have probably heard.

"There stood a medical officer and made signs with his thumb. Left meant life and right meant death; only we didn't know that at the time. Though I wanted to go to the right side, to follow a friend of mine, he sent me to the left.

"All the children - and there were many and beautiful ones - with their young mothers, and the weak and the old people, were sent to the right side.

"When we entered the gates and I saw endless rows of barracks closed on electric wires, I didn't believe I would ever get out alive. Then, they led us to a bath, where we had to undress. [They] cut our hair everywhere, and gave us some dirty rags and wooden slippers.

"And now began a life that seems to me like a nightmare, no, worse, for my poor brain could never have invented such things.

"But I was lucky. After a week, already we were selected for work and sent to Freiberg in Saxonia.

"We worked there in a factory for 8 months - hard work, little sleep and less food, only one dress, one pair of sneakers, one chemise [undergarment], no stockings. In February, I got a pair. And yet it was paradise compared to Auschwitz.

"The worst thing was that I didn't know anything of Gerd. But I was convinced that he would survive it. And this thought helped me to endure everything.

"After all I heard later, he wasn't even given a chance to survive it; he must have been sent to the wrong side immediately. I can't yet understand it.

"There were many who after 8 months of a h--- of a life were dying of hunger. In this case, it was better to find an end at once, that is my only consolation, and yet - but there is no use in speaking about that.

"When the front was quite near, the Germans packed us in coal wagons, with coal dust an inch thick, and for days and days we were on the road, never knowing where we were going, 60 to 100 people in one wagon, starving.

"On the 13th day, I escaped near Klatovy. The others still went for three days to Mauthausen concentration camp, where we were to be gassed. I was hiding in a small village for 14 days.

"Then the Americans came and I could go to Prague, sure Gerd would be already waiting for me. It was a wonderful thing to have a bath, to sleep in a clean bed, to eat as much as you like. I ate enormous quantities.

"But it wasn't the homecoming I had expected. Everyone you had known - and loved - gone. A strange town.

"Now I have a flat, I am teaching as before, earning my living quite decently. I am even laughing and joking, and most people think I am leading a content life.

"Here you have the whole story. If you want to know more, ask me; this time, I will answer promptly. It was only the first letter that was so hard to write. You don't know how glad I was to get news from you and to know there are people out to whom you somehow belong.

"Write to me soon about your life and your kids. I am so glad you have them. If it is possible, send me photos. Much love. Yours, Gerta."

Behind the letter was an official-looking document. "Dear Friend," it started, "Upon your request, we have effected the necessary inquiry and, according to our card index of all inhabitants of the Terezin ghetto, we have found the following data concerning the persons in question:

"Mr. Friedrich [Fritz] Eidlitz [the grandmother's father], last residence Prague, was deported 2.7.1942 with transport AA1-651 to Terezin, and 15.10.1942 with transport BV-1499 to Treblinka - did not return.

"Mrs. Ida Eidlitz [the grandmother's mother], last residence Prague, was deported 2.7.1942 with transport AA1-652 to Terezin, and 15.10.1942 with transport BV-1500 to Treblinka. She did not return.

"Mr. Friedel Schlosser [youthful cousin to the grandmother, who went voluntarily to the death camps in order to accompany his grandparents], last residence Prague, was deported 13.5.1943 with transport DB-28 to Terezin, and 6.9.1943 with transport DM-3189 to Auschwitz - did not return.

"Mr. Oskar Scholosser [Friedel's grandfather and Gerd's father], last residence Prague, was deported 27.7.1942 with transport AAu-502 to Terezin, and 6.9.1943 with transport DM-3161 to Auschwitz. Did not return.

"Mrs. Marta Scholosser [Friedel's grandmother and Gerd's mother], last residence Prague, was deported 27.7.1942 with transport AAu-501 to Terezin, and 6.9.1943 with transport DM-3160 to Auschwitz - did not return.

"Mr. Gerhard [Gerd] Schlosser, last residence Prague, was deported 30.1.1942 with transport V-635 to Terezin, and 28.9.1944 with transport EK-2497 to Auschwitz - did not return.

"Each of them was taken away in a different transport car, and probably went to the gas chamber alone," my friend said, "and met that terrible death - of not being able to breathe - without a family member to comfort them."

She shook her head, and then cried.

"All of these people," she concluded, "who my grandmother loved ...."

To be continued.

Postscript:

My father had visited many of the places described in these articles, and spoke affectedly after reading them.

"It was interesting," he began. "Talking about the people who stayed and who left, and it must have been terribly, terribly difficult for Jews in the ghetto and places like that – it's hard to even try to imagine how difficult it must have been."

"You remember Denny," he continued. Denny was my father's friend from Czechoslavakia, who had recently returned to that country. "His father was a doctor in Prague, and when the Germans came, his friends who were Jewish gave him the Torahs to store up in his attic during the war.

"And there were all kinds of situations there. A lot of Jewish children were put with Catholic families during the war year in farms out in the countryside. Unfortunately, a lot of times the parents didn't come home."

"When I went to visit Denny in Prague," he concluded, "we went to an old Jewish synagogue and it was really interesting - what was done. I think there was a lot of compassion among the friends of a lot of the Jewish families who realized what was going on, and did everything they could to make life somewhat bearable, and hid them, kept them, because they knew what the alternative was going to be..."

CHAPTER TEN

Part IV, The letter from the Holocaust: Grieving the Dead.
Michael Yanuck
Waxing Philosophical
The Paris Post-Intelligencer, Paris, Tenn., Page 2, March 27, 2009.

While snowed in at the home of a friend's grandmother, I came across a box of papers that included a letter that documented the fate of her family in the Holocaust.

By morning of the following day, the roads had been mostly cleared, so that my friend's mother was able to join us at the grandmother's. It was then that we shared the contents of the box, especially the Holocaust letter. My friend's mother read it, tearfully.

"This letter affected me, too," the mother said. "After my mother received it, she was so stricken by grief that she took to her bed, and wasn't able to care for me for almost a year. I was 3 years old then, and all I remember was the sound of her crying."

The mother asked if I understood the significance of the grandmother's hand-written note about Sudetenland. I read the note again.

"Can you go home again?" it said. "1933 Hitler elected. 1938 Austria. Sept. 1938 Munich - Chamberlain - "peace in our time" - Sudetenland. Jan. 18, 1939, we left. March 15, 1939, Hitler in Prague."

"I suppose that it represents your mother's way of recounting the critical events leading to World War II," I said.

She shook her head. "It wasn't really about that, Mike," the mother said. "The Munich agreement was terrible for the world, but actually provided the way for my mom to get out of Europe.

"You see, her husband - my dad - had been born in Sudetenland. When Chamberlain signed the pact with Hitler that handed the Sudetenland over to the Nazis, it automatically put the Jews there at risk. That meant that they could apply for visas to the United States, and get out.

"The rest of the Jews in Czechoslovakia couldn't do that, because they weren't considered at risk from Hitler - not until it was too late.

"No one else on my mother's side of the family had a connection to Sudetenland - only my mother because of her marriage to my father.

"There was actually a very narrow window for my mom and dad to get out. It was only a couple of months between the Munich agreement and the time when Hitler invaded Czechoslovakia.

"But my dad foresaw what was coming. He'd been a student in Germany for a time - and been thrown down a flight of stairs. So, when he got the chance to leave Europe, he took it in a hurry.

"That's how my mother became the only blood relative from her family to survive."

In another note written some 40 years after the Holocaust letter, the grandmother described a service in honor of her loved ones:

"On April 22, 1995, we will dedicate a Torah scroll with many names of victims of the Holocaust. Thirteen of these names have a special significance for me and my children.

"They are the names of members of my immediate family: my parents, my grandmother, my aunts and uncles and my cousins, who all perished in the death camps of the Holocaust.

"My parents, Dr. Friedrich Eidlitz and Ida Eidlitz, in their 70s, were deported to Treblinka in 1942 just around the time when I had my first child.

"My cousin Herta Bloch, her husband Emil Bloch and their little boy, Hansi, age 10, were taken to Auschwitz, as were all the others. My favorite cousin, Gerd Schlosser, playmate of my childhood, perished in Auschwitz shortly before the end of the war.

"There are no graves to mark their place of rest. Their bodies were burned to ashes ...."

"During the night, my grandma tells me that she still sees the faces of her family," my friend said. "At times, my grandma says she looks at me, and is reminded of them. She says it's because I look at lot like the people in her family who she lost.

"I don't think Grandma's ever come to terms with the way they met their end," she continued. "When my sister was in high school, she wanted to participate in a certain Holocaust program.

"It was called, 'The Death March,' and involved walking between the different concentration camps in Europe, and ended in Auschwitz.

"My parents didn't have the money to pay for it, so my sister went to my grandma and asked for her support. Grandma had always encouraged us to learn about the world, and would, at times, help finance our travels.

"But this time, Grandma refused. She was adamant, and insisted that my sister not go on this trip, saying that the only thing she'd find there was death and graves."

To be continued.

CHAPTER ELEVEN

Part V, The letter from the Holocaust: Coming to terms with the past.
Michael Yanuck
Waxing Philosophical
The Paris Post-Intelligencer, Paris, Tenn., Page 2, March 27, 2009.

I agonized quite a bit before submitting this concluding piece for the Holocaust Letter series. Really, I was quite taken aback by Barr's response to the series, and resolved to take any direct personal thoughts out of my writing, and just let the story be told by those who lived it.

But there was still something that I wanted to say, and when I shared my angst with a reader-friend, he wrote the following:

"Dear Mike, I am glad you are using the format of the PI for the Holocaust series. I cannot remember (not that my memory is very reliable) an article in recent years devoted exclusively to the Holocaust. Although it makes us 'wince' and tempts us to turn away, it is a true story that needs to be told. By Sara's willingness to share and your willingness to write, you are personalizing the Holocaust in a way that catches our attention. It is one thing to share facts (which in and of itself is also important), but when a personal letter is shared you catch the emotional import of the writer and catch a glimpse of what they must have been feeling. The fact that the letter involves someone the writer knows personally also strengthens the impact of the story. It is not about someone far away, but someone you know (Sara's grandmother). As for how the subject should be expressed (through the story of individuals or spoken outright), why not both. Complete your story via the individuals and then give a synopsis

expressing your points outright and why you feel this story has an importance for today's readers. I for one have enjoyed them because it sparks internal reflection over a horrible period of human history. This reflection may not be fun, but it is needed if one is to learn the lessons history has to teach..."

What follows was directly inspired by this reader.

While snowed-in at the home of a friend's grandmother, I came across a box of forgotten papers that documented the fate of her family who had perished in the Holocaust.

Although the grandmother had once voiced an opinion that her offspring never visit the concentration camps of Europe - and that all they'd find there was "graves" - sorting through the box, I found a letter that suggested that the grandmother's feeling towards her homeland had softened. It was dated 7-12-93, and written to my friend (her grand-daughter):

"I understand that you are thinking of spending a few days in Prague on you way home from Israel," the grandmother wrote. "I think that you will find Prague to be a beautiful city with both an ancient past and a vibrant present.

"With your artist's eye you will appreciate the beautiful architecture of many of the century old buildings and you will love the hustle and bustle of the modern city with its tourists from all of Europe, especially teenagers and young people camping all over the city.

"You will love to listen to the street singers who set up camp on the sidewalks with their guitars, sing old and new songs and ask for donation. You will love to walk along the big river called Vltava or Moldau as I and your grandpa Richard used to do every night.

"You will go to the square in the old city and watch the famous clock with beats every hour and the 12 apostles appear and march around waving. The gruesome story of the clock tells that the inventor was blinded by the king so he would not be able to make another clock just like it.

"You will go to the old Jewish cemetery where the grave stones are put one on top of the other because the graves are placed up to 10 layers deep in the limited space and you will visit the 500 year old synagogue.

"You will see the statue of the famous Rabbi Loew, the legendary creator of the Golem, supposedly an ancestor of your grandfather Richard.

"You will visit the 1000 year old castle of the Czech kings which dominates the city and you will go to the gathering place for painters and other artists who work there. However, wear a money belt under your clothes for your valuables! It is also a gathering place for pickpockets!

"You will meet Gerta Schlosser who was married to my cousin Gerd and who is the only survivor of my family. She is about 85 and partially blind but she is very alert, speaks good English and will love to see you.

"Have a wonderful time in my old playground! Love from grandma."

Before leaving the house, I asked the grandmother if I might one day write about her family's experience, and publish her letters.

"The letters are personal," she said in a breathless voice, "but you can print them - though I don't know why anyone would be interested in what happened to my family..."

As for my interest, I suppose that I could say I wanted to document the experiences of this small group of loving individuals who were systematically treated in the cruelest of ways.

But, really, I was touched by these letters. Their human quality shines through, and provides a glimpse of what it was to live through one of the darkest periods in recorded history.

Then, I read an article attacking Muslim immigrants, and felt differently about this story; it appears that even in this day in age when we've lived to see the election of our first African American President, we still cannot take for granted that all understand that people of every race, creed and religion are entitled to be looked upon as equals, governed by laws, and that no group should be slated for attack.

I cannot imagine what it feels like to be a Muslim in this country, where you are openly and publicly attacked because hate-filled radicals of your religion were responsible for 9/11. It's equivalent to referring to all Southerners as bigots and murders because of the actions of the Ku Klux Klan.

Placing the grandmother's letters back in the card-board box from which they came, I stumbled upon a final note - this one titled, "An important day in my life":

"It was January 26, 1939. I was in the cabin of the French ocean liner Isle de France, lying on my bed desperately sea-sick.

"It had been a very rough crossing on the stormy Atlantic. I had been sea-sick most of the 6 days since we had left the coast of France.

"I was traveling with my husband to the United States, leaving our old life behind and embarking on a new and exciting adventure.

"It had been a difficult decision to leave my native Czechoslovakia. We had a happy and fulfilling life in Prague, the beautiful Capital of our country. I was a teacher and law student and my husband was establishing his medical practice as a pediatrician. We had a large and loving family consistent of parents, brothers and sisters and many aunts, uncles and cousins.

"Leaving the country was an idea which was furthest from our minds. But the clouds of war and political upheaval were closing in on our peaceful democracy and many of our friends were preparing to leave.

"Young and adventurous as we were, we decided to go away for a short while and return when the political situation improved. This was a very naïve and simplistic idea. We did not anticipate that we would never see our family again. That a devastating war was going to engulf Europe and that 50 years would pass before I would again set foot on the beautiful ancient city of Prague.

"As I was lying in the cabin, sick, and feverish, I heard a noisy commotion outside, cries of, 'There she is,' and, 'Look how tall she is.'

"The ship was shaking violently in the heavy surf and I had to make a great effort to get out of bed and climb upstairs on to the deck. I had seen many pictures of the Statue of Liberty but I was not prepared to see it close up silhouetted against the New York skyline. It was an awesome and exciting view.

"We finally landed in a heavy winter storm and started our new life in a new land, with a new language and new friends, but I never forgot that first impression of the United States with the great Statue in New York harbor greeting us with outstretched arms of welcome."

Postscript: Ultimately, my fiancee insisted I remove the section about the treatment of Muslim immigrants. I felt that this weakened the impact of the piece, but, as this was her family's story, I had to respect her wishes. When I confided this to my reader-friend, he responded this way:

"Dear Mike, I still think the piece will have an impact on those who read it and certainly have implications for us today. The Holocaust is something that many of us (especially who have lived our entire lives in the rural South) have heard and read about, but have not had personal contact with those who either went through it themselves or had family members that had gone through it. Because you are known in Paris (via a past member of the health care community here and a contributor to the PI for some time), you are our link to Sara's grandmother. Again, thanks to Sara's grandmother, Sara, and her family for allowing you to print these letters. It puts a "face" on a grim time in world history, and hopefully as people read

it, they will come away saying that should never happen again and that just because someone is of a different race or creed they should still be treated with dignity..."

CHAPTER TWELVE

Holocaust survivor on deathbed.
Michael
Yanuck
Waxing Philosophical
The Paris Post-Intelligencer, Paris, Tenn, Page 2, October 17th, 2009.

   Upon hearing of her grandmother's declining condition, my
friend rushed to her grandmother's side.
   I accompanied my friend. It's 4 in the morning now, and family
is still arriving.
   "I don't know where I would have been without her," a
grandson says.
   The grandson holds his grandmother's hand, and then whispers,
"We love you, Grandma."
   In her delirium, the grandmother speaks to her long-departed
father in German.
   The grandson looks at me, surprised. "Do you realize that she
hasn't spoken that language since the War?" he says.
   After learning of the murder of her family at the hands of the
Nazis [previously described in the "Letter from the Holocaust"
series, March 6-April 3], the grandmother had vowed never to speak
German again.
   Before that, the grandmother regularly conversed in that
language, and even worked with Sigmund Freud to translate his
writings from German into Czech.
   "I think that she might be coming to terms with the past," the
grandson continues.

I resist the impulse to tell him no, and that it's only the confluence of her numerous medical maladies - including anemia, infection and multi-organ failure - that have caught up with his grandmother, and left her in a confused and altered mental state.

"I want to go home!" the grandmother calls out. "Help me go home!"

My friend stays by her grandmother's side. Two days later, she has not slept.

Awakening on the morning of the third day of the grandmother's vigil, I find my friend in the same place where I'd left her the night before.

There's a certain glow that seems to emanate from my friend and, whereas I'm shaking off the vestiges of sleep, my friend looks somehow refreshed.

"I just don't want her to feel alone," my friend says. "I want her to know that she's loved."

"The grandmother could never have been alone," I think silently. Even if the grandmother had been a thousand miles away, my friend's heart still would have found her, to surround her with an aura of love.

Then, my friend turns to me. "Mike, what do you think is happening inside Grandma's body?" she asks.

As I begin to deliberate, I perform some subtle exams. Checking the grandmother's pulse, I notice that it feels thready and notably different than the night before.

Then, I look up, and see that the grandmother's pattern of breathing has abruptly changed.

I move forward and hold my friend, and tell her to prepare herself, because the moment of her grandmother's passing is near at hand.

My friend asks if there's time to alert the other family members.

I tell her no, and it's just the three of us now.

(To be continued.)

CHAPTER THIRTEEN

Caregivers can be a blessing.
Michael Yanuck
Waxing Philosophical
The Paris Post-Intelligencer, Paris, Tenn, Page 2, October 23rd, 2009.

At the bedside of my friend's 97-year-old grandmother, a survivor of the Holocaust, I noticed a change in her breathing.

Then, within the span of three breaths, the flame that had burned so long finally went out.

Within a moment of the grandmother's passing, her primary caregiver, Lisa, enters the room.

"What's happened?" Lisa says. "Hold on, Bubby! I have to get your daughters down here first!"

After making some urgent calls, Lisa runs back into the room, kneels and weeps over the grandmother's body.

In the weeks before, Lisa and I had clashed over the grandmother's care. It began when the grandmother fell ill before a family wedding.

I insisted that an ambulance be called, but Lisa and the other caregivers were opposed, saying that it was the grandmother's wish to remain at home, and not be taken to the hospital.

I was incensed. "What is wrong with these women?" I thought. "Don't they know that this woman staying alive is their livelihood? When she dies, they have to pack up and find another job! Don't they understand that? Keep her alive!"

Fortunately, with the help of some antibiotics, the grandmother recovered.

Then, on the eve of the wedding, Lisa called me again, saying that the grandmother, Marietta, had had a difficult night, and asking me to come to the home.

"Mike, you don't know what's been going on here," Lisa said. "Marietta's biological clock is all thrown off. She sleeps during the day, and then keeps me up all night, hollering and screaming and asking for all kinds of stuff. I'm at my wits' end."

This condition is called 'terminal restlessness,' and I instructed Lisa to give the grandmother a sedative so that both of them could get some rest.

"No, Mike!" she responded. "I don't want to drug her up! If I do that, she won't be awake for the wedding!"

She shook her head. "Mike, I want you to know that I appreciate everything you did for Marietta," Lisa said. "The medicine that you prescribed got her past that bad bout of pneumonia, and I'm grateful to you for that.

"But I was very hurt by some of the things you said …. Michael, for the past months, that wedding is all she's been living for. It's all she talks about.

"But she doesn't want to go to the hospital. I agree with you that that's the place for sick people, but she's had some bad experiences there, and she's afraid of that place.

"You might think that you know best, but I spend more time with that woman than anyone. I bathe her, I clothe her, I sing to her, I wipe her after she's gone to the potty.

"I listen to that woman, Michael. It's not just, 'Here's your tea, sweety. Now, let me put you in bed.' I've crossed all the boundaries that I'm not supposed to.

"And maybe I butt in where I'm not supposed to, but it's been three years that I've cared for that woman, and I want her wishes respected."

The following day the grandmother came for the wedding. I expected her to sleep through the ceremony; but to my surprise, she was awake.

Then, she was awake for a second ceremony involving the marriage of a second granddaughter. Then, she was awake for the reception.

Even as the event neared its end, the grandmother was still awake, and actively conversing with yet another granddaughter, who had flown in from California.

"She wanted to be there," a grandson said. "She willed herself. It meant a lot to her."

Perhaps, it did, but probably more responsible for this feat than anyone or anything else was Lisa and the grandmother's other caregivers.

They had not only selflessly put the grandmother's wishes ahead of their own livelihoods, but took it upon themselves to pull the grandmother through - staying up with the grandmother through the night, rather than sedating her with pills so that they could rest comfortably.

The grandmother's caregivers were not family, and could even be described as strangers who came into the grandmother's life at the end.

All of the grandmother's contemporary family members had perished at the hands of strangers - gassed in the concentration camps of Auschwitz and Treblinka.

It is therefore a source of great hope that caregivers such as those who attended to the grandmother still exist in the world.

And that caring for another should be more than a job, but an act of giving of oneself.

CHAPTER FOURTEEN

Honoring the composers of the Terezín ghetto on Holocaust Remembrance Day.

Despite continued efforts to distance myself from Holocaust stories, I keep being pulled back.

"Mike, the people who lived through the Holocaust are dying off," a reader told me. "If you don't document their stories, they might never be told."

In light of this reader's encouragement and recent events involving the fatal shooting at the Holocaust Museum, I'd like to offer one more piece. This is a story about Holocaust Remembrance Day:

When I read that The Grateful Dead were playing nearby, I made plans to attend.

Then, my friend's mother announced that it was "Holocaust Remembrance Day," and suggested an event featuring music composed at the Terezin Ghetto, where her family had been interned before sent to the death camps.

The tickets were not inexpensive.

"Seems like a lot of money for a depressing evening," I thought.

After all, not one of the composers of the selection to be played survived the Holocaust.

But I felt I had to do something to observe the Remembrance Day, and paid for the tickets.

The event was held in a church, and, scanning those in attendance, I didn't see many Jewish faces.

Certainly, the performers weren't Jewish. The singer was

40

Swedish. The violinist English. What did they know about the Holocaust experience?

Sitting through the opening compositions, I found the music haunting. It spoke to feelings of the sadness, hopelessness and desperation. When the intermission came, I greeted it with relief.

But my friend's mother confided that she was happy we'd come.

"It makes me feel good to know that if the members of my family had to be in that dreadful place, at least they had music," she said.

The music resumed, and I felt as though teleported to the ghetto itself, and with each musical score I felt more and more connected with the fate of my long departed brethren.

It was as if I were right there with them, trapped in the ghetto, or riding in those transport trains to the death camps.

"Line me up, and shoot me where I stand," I thought. "Or put me into a gas chamber, and then burn my flesh to ashes. But, God willing, let me live a righteous life."

And then, when all seemed lost and no hope left, the concert ended, and those in attendance at the church stood and applauded.

And I stood, too - but it was mostly to acknowledge those all around me who cared enough to honor the murdered composers, so that their works would endure, their cause remembered, and their spirit saved for all the ages.

CHAPTER FIFTEEN

Hanne is a quiet witness to love.
Michael Yanuck
Waxing Philosophical
The Paris Post-Intelligencer, Paris, Tenn., Page 2, December 30th,
2009.

During the holidays, I was asked to help transport an older
cousin to a family gathering.

Her name was Hanne, and she was about 80 years old and
confined to a wheelchair.

When I got to her home, Hanne apologized for her difficulties in
moving and getting into the car.

But none of these apologies was necessary, as I was deeply
moved by her strenuous efforts to be with her family.

Then, at the chosen site of the gathering, Hanne had to ascend a
flight of stairs. Again, she apologized for her difficulties, but assisting
her was as though no effort at all, as I could only marvel at her
willingness to exert such reserves of energy to be among loved ones.

Now, surrounded by family, Hanne sat smiling through the
festivities. Given that she was really at the mercy of others to assist
her, I was struck by her patience and good cheer.

"Do you know Hanne's story?" my mother-in-law asked. "Well,
since my mother died, Hanne is the sole surviving member of the
family who lived through the Holocaust. Her life was somewhat like
Anne Frank's. ... She grew up a hidden child."

"Hanne's father was a German soldier," she continued. "Her
mother was Jewish. The two separated as he became more
militaristic and fell in step with the Fascists.

"After he was sent off to the war, Hanne's mother was in danger of being sent to a concentration camp (which she eventually was), so the father's parents invited Hanne to stay with them.

"But keeping Hanne was putting them in danger (or, at least, in an uncomfortable position), and the father's parents began making sounds that they would send Hanne back to her mom, which would have meant death for her.

"So an aunt (her mom's sister) took Hanne. The story goes that the aunt carried Hanne off in the middle of the night and ran away with her.

"The aunt and her Christian husband took Hanne with them to Switzerland, where the Christian husband kept the aunt and Hanne hidden for the rest of the war, and saved them.

"Both Hanne's parents died. Her dad died while fighting on the front; her mom in a concentration camp.

"After the war, the aunt and uncle emigrated to the United States and, again, took Hanne with them. Hanne was viewed as their daughter, and they lived together as a family.

"Then, when Hanne became a young woman, she fell in love with a man named Gil.

"But Gil was Puerto Rican, and the aunt and uncle opposed Hanne seeing him because they thought he was beneath her.

"You'd think that the aunt and uncle would have known better … known how damaging bigotry was in any form. All that misery in the Holocaust. All those deaths, just because one group didn't want to accept another.

"But they continued to insist that Hanne have nothing to do with Gil - so Hanne and Gil eloped, and lived happily ever after.

"Well, that's not completely true. Hanne developed multiple sclerosis and, throughout her life, suffered bouts of that disease, which left her incapacitated. Gil was always good to her, though, and saw her through all that.

"Then, Gil developed Alzheimer's disease. When he lost his mental capacities, Hanne cared for him to the end."

Gazing across the room, my eyes fell on Hanne. Incapacitated, but still smiling, she is a quiet witness to love, heroism, the ability to overcome and the promise of a better world.

CHAPTER SIXTEEN

Hanne's survival depended on Germans, like Rudulf.
Michael Yanuck
Waxing Philosophical
The Paris Post-Intelligencer, Paris, Tenn., Page 2, January 7th, 2010.

In last week's column, I presented a short glimpse of a Holocaust survivor named Hanne.

An older woman now bound to a wheelchair, she had survived World War II because she had been hidden from the Nazis by a Christian uncle.

The events of Hanne's rescue had been related by family members. I would have liked to ask Hanne myself, but had been told that she wasn't inclined to talk about her experience.

Then, the following day, we got a call that Hanne was being taken to the emergency room.

"Hanne has a bad infection in her leg," Hanne's caregiver said. "She said that she hurt her leg a couple of days ago. I think that she must have bumped into a table while she was getting around in her wheelchair, and took off some of the skin.

"The wound is all red and swollen. I asked her if she told anyone about it, but she said that she didn't want to be a bother, and that's why she hadn't said anything before.

"I called her doctor, and she was insistent that I take Hanne to the hospital to get the wound looked at."

Arriving at the hospital, I examined Hanne's leg. It was inflamed and tender, and I felt sad that I hadn't seen it the day before and offered treatment.

"It's just a scratch," Hanne said. "I didn't want to waste your time over it."

But her caregiver continued to express concern.

"This was the first time that I've been to Hanne's in three months," the caregiver said. "It was only because her other caregiver, Annie, is still visiting with her mother for Christmas.

"Annie doesn't have any medical training or experience, so I imagine that's why she didn't notice the wound or give it much thought. I guess it was just lucky that I was around to see it."

Then, the caregiver smiled broadly.

"Everything happens for a reason," the caregiver said, cheerfully. "That's what I always say."

Listening, I couldn't help but wonder what Hanne thought of her caregiver's last statement, seeing that Hanne had lived through one of the worst periods in human history - a time that seemed to offer very little "reason" for its happenings.

"Well, I have to leave now," the caregiver said. "I have some clients at a group home that I have to check in on. I'll call tomorrow to see how things went here."

The caregiver departed, and we waited with Hanne in the emergency room.

"I'm sorry that you felt like you needed to come out here," Hanne said. "It's really nothing. I'm sure that it will get better on its own."

After getting Hanne situated in a room in the Emergency Department with blood work performed and treatment started, it was suggested that I go to the gym and work out.

"Yes, go," Hanne said. "Have fun."

Maybe that was a good idea, I thought, as I hadn't exercised in a while.

But, rising to my feet, I realized that, really, I didn't want to leave.

"I'm a sucker for a story," I told Hanne. "And from what I understand, you've had an interesting life."

"No, nothing interesting about me," Hanne said. "But, if you want to know something, you can feel free to ask."

I nodded, and then edged closer.

"How did you get by," I asked, "while in hiding during World War II?"

"My aunt supported us," she said. "She was an artist, and made painted plates that my uncle would sell. My uncle would arrange with the local farmers to bring us the wood and raw materials that she used to make decorative wood plates and paint them.

"We'd sit - all of us - by a large stove, and work all day, painting those bowls.

"The stove roared all day, but it was still always cold inside, because we were on the second floor and there was always all that snow.

"Then, my uncle would carry a package of these plates to the local ski resorts in the surrounding villages. This was around Innsbrook in Austria, where many tourists came to ski. They'd purchase my aunt's bowls, so that we could make money.

"That's how we survived the war. That's how we made our money. If it hadn't been for those Nazi tourists, we wouldn't have been able to stay alive."

How did your aunt and uncle pick this place in Austria to live out the war?

"Well, my aunt and uncle were both from Prague, where their families lived, but my uncle saw what was coming, and made it his mission to save my family.

"He was German, but he really liked my aunt's side of the family, and that was an important reason why he tried to do as much as he could.

"My uncle's father was the chief of police in Prague, so he could use those connections to find out what was up.

"It actually saved my aunt and him because the police came to him before the Gestapo. They told him that the Gestapo had discovered that his wife was Jewish, and were coming to take them away.

"That very night, he and my aunt disappeared into Austria.

"But he left behind a contact for me, a man named Rudolf, who I was to go to if I saw that things were getting bad. And when things got worse, I went to Rudolf."

Where were you at the time?

"My uncle had made a plan to send me to my father's father, where he thought I would be safe. Through his connections, he knew that it wouldn't be long before my mother was sent to the concentration camp.

"He knew that if I went with her, I probably wouldn't last long, because in the concentration camps, it was the children and the old people who were usually the first to go - transferred to other camps where no one ever came back, or were never heard from again.

"My father's father took me, but I don't think that he was very happy about it. He was on the other side. I guess that I really can't blame him, because I was putting them in danger. If the Gestapo would have found out that he was harboring me, then it would have made some serious trouble for them.

"I could tell that things were getting worse. That's when I told Rudolf, and he relayed the message to my aunt and uncle in Austria."

To be continued.

Postscript:

As well as publishing Hanne's story in the P-I, I was also sharing it with friends and family. One of the most meaningful response that I received came from a family friend, who captured the essence of what writing could mean when she wrote the following:

"HI, MIKE, I read thru this and was much moved to think about how the action of individuals made all the difference between Life and Death for Dvora's cousin. The fact that you have made a written record of it is ALSO significant, as it SAVES her LIFE (story) for a second time, for posterity. Your writing enlarges on the essence of your career as a medical doctor......in a most poetic way. Hanne now will have a chance at eternal life....something most of us are not given. Claire."

CHAPTER SEVENTEEN

Part III: Hanne goes to Austria.
Michael Yanuck
Waxing Philosophical
The Paris Post-Intelligencer, Paris, Tenn., Page 2, January 15th, 2010.

Hanne, an older woman who survived the Holocaust during World War II as a hidden child, now required treatment in the hospital for an infection.

Although usually reticent about describing her experience, she agreed to talk about it.

We rejoin her story at the point when her aunt and uncle begin their journey to rescue her.

"My aunt and uncle took big risks in coming to get me," Hanne said. "In those days, you couldn't travel more than 10 miles from your home, or else you could be arrested.

"Where they were in Austria was far away from the Sudenland (where she was with her father's father). So they had to be very careful. If someone had asked for their passport on a train, it might have been it for them.

"But they came. I think that the reason why they took me was because my grandfather said that he was going to send me back to my mother. It was partly my fault.

"I was seven years old at the time and, like any other kid, I wanted to be with my mother. I made the mistake of telling my grandfather that, and he was saying that he was going to send me back.

"So my aunt and uncle came back that night, and took me away with them to Austria. At the time, they were living in a little town near Innsbrook called St. Jacob.

"They were renting from a landlady, who had pretended that she was anti-Nazi. But she wasn't, and the reason why we had to leave there was my fault.

"I became friends with the landlady's niece. She was about my age - a little older, perhaps. I suppose that I wanted someone to confide to.

"One day, I made the mistake of telling her that I was Jewish, and hiding with my aunt and uncle because all of my family in Prague was being taken away and sent to concentration camps.

"Well, they informed on us. When the Gestapo man in town came to the house, I had to say that I had lied, and made the whole thing up, and it was just that my childhood imagination had gone wild and got the best of me.

"After the interview, the Gestapo man told my uncle that it was all right, and he wasn't going to report us or make any further inquiries.

"Still, in the middle of a snow storm not long after, we collected all our belongings and left the village for good.

"My uncle bought tickets for a city far away that would have taken days on train to get to. But really, we were only on the train for two hours before we got off at a different village.

"And, the truth was, this didn't fool anyone. After the war, the Gestapo man told us that he knew exactly where we went after we left St. Jacob.

"But he never turned us in, and - the truth is - we could never be sure why. Maybe he was acting out of the goodness of his heart - I don't know.

"Hitler had already seen a number of losses by that time, and the people working for him had an idea that the war was coming to an end, and it wasn't looking good for them.

"And they might need something to show that they weren't completely with the Nazis - give them an excuse to say that they weren't all bad.

"So, who knows? Maybe, we were the Gestapo man's excuse?"

To be continued.

CHAPTER EIGHTEEN

Part 4: Hanne's uncle takes action.
Michael Yanuck
Waxing Philosophical
The Paris Post-Intelligencer, Paris, Tenn., Page 2, January 22nd, 2010.

Hanne, an older woman who survived the Holocaust during World War II as a hidden child, describes her and her relatives seeking another place of hiding in Austria.

"At the other village," she said, "my uncle had arranged for us to rent a place from a farmer.

"It was on the second floor, and had a big stove that was always roaring. But because of all the ice and snow outside, it was still always cold there, and you never could get warm.

"There wasn't much to do. When I wasn't working, I would go outside. There was really no one to talk to.

"I couldn't go to school, because that would mean checking my identification, and, if they found out who I really was, then it would be the end for me.

"So if anybody asked, I would say that I was fourteen and had completed my schooling. Actually, I was only ten, really.

"Mostly, it all seemed like a terrible nightmare that I kept wishing I could just wake up from.

"Even after the war ended, you could never be sure that problems wouldn't start again. And for some people, things got worse.

"That's the way it was for my uncle's family, because they were

Germans living in Czechoslovakia. After the war, when the Russians came into Czechoslovakia, they rounded up all the Germans living there and marched them to camps in Siberia.

"This is what happened to my uncle's remaining family, his mother and his brother. Once they were taken away, they were never heard from again.

"I think that's why my uncle came to this country - because, after all that, he couldn't bear to be in Europe any longer.

"But it was never the same as before. My aunt and uncle had lost all their belongings, all their friends. And the war took such a toll on my uncle's health.

"For the rest of his life, my uncle suffered from a heart condition that never got better. He had lots of chest pain, and would have to spend days in bed.

"I think it was from all the times that he had to move in the cold between those villages in the mountains of Austria - finding places to sell my aunt's plates, and communicating with associates in the underground. And I'm sure that needing to take care of me didn't help, either.

"My aunt and uncle never did have children. My uncle didn't want them. I think that it was because he thought humans were on a downward phase, and the end was near for them.

"He was a realist, and saw things for what they were, and I don't think that he had a lot of hope for humans.

"Still, to my aunt, my uncle was always a hero. She never uttered one bad word about him, and worshipped the ground he walked on.

"But I don't think that my uncle really felt that he had accomplished much. After all, as well as losing all of my aunt's family to the war - that is, besides my aunt and me - afterwards, he lost all of his family, too.

"When I remember him now, I think that my uncle was a person like everyone else. Most people don't want to see others getting hurt or mistreated.

"I guess that he was just a little better than most because he acted on it."

To be continued.

Postscript:
At about this point in the story, Hanne had to excuse herself. As we sat waiting, my wife quietly reflected.

"It's interesting," my wife began. "The sisters both got married, and Hanne's mom had a kid [Hanne]. And when the winds turned

(like to way they're turning right now), there was pressure on German guys married to Jewish women to renounce their marriages.

"And Hanne's dad did that: He renounced his marriage to his wife, and then he signed up for the German Army and he became a soldier. And on the other side, her sister's husband, Renee, did not renounce his marriage to his wife: He stayed with her. And, in fact, because of his father's contacts with the Czech police from when his father was alive, he was in contact with high up police officials and when things were going to turn really bad for the Jews of Prague, the police came to Renee and told him they were going to come and collect Jews, because they knew his wife was Jewish. So Renee found a village in the Swiss Alps and took his wife and hid her there.

"Hanne's mom was taken to a concentration camp, but Hanne was left in the apartment by herself until her German grandfather came and took her. But there was pressure on him. So the German grandfather contacted Renee that it was no longer safe for Hanne to stay with him and he didn't know what to do. Soon Renee came and took Hanne, and took her to where they were hiding and kept her hidden for the whole war.

"But when the Russians entered Prague after the war, they took Renee's German family and exiled them to Siberia, and they were never heard of again. So, Renee sticking by his Jewish wife and sheltering her through the war in the Austrian Alps had saved him from being taken with the rest of his family to Siberia.

"It's like love can take you in ways places that can save you when you thought that they wouldn't."

CHAPTER NINETEEN

Part 5: Fate of Hanne's parents.
Michael Yanuck
Waxing Philosophical
The Paris Post-Intelligencer, Paris, Tenn., Page 2, January 28th, 2010.

Hanne, an older woman who during World War II had survived the Holocaust as a hidden child, now required treatment in the hospital for an infection.

Although usually reticent about describing her experience, she had agreed to talk about it. I asked what became of her father, who had been a German soldier.

"My father was reported as missing in action after the battle of Stalingrad," Hanne said. "Another soldier who knew my father (and fought there) said that when they pulled back, my father wasn't among them.

"He probably died there. I don't know. I never heard anything about him after that.

"He actually got remarried during one of his last furloughs, and his wife had a son. I heard this from my grandfather.

"It was in the last letter that my grandfather sent me. He asked if I wanted to meet my brother.

"I never replied to that letter. I'm not sure why. I was pretty young at the time, and I think that I was probably confused, and maybe just wanted to cut off my relationship with that side of my family.

"I think that the marriage between my father and this woman had probably been arranged, and that side was going the other way (toward the Fascists), and I couldn't imagine that I would have a lot in common with my brother."

Do you remember your father?

"No," Hanne said. "I was probably four years old when he left, and I have no memory of him."

How did your parents meet?

"They met in music school," she said. "My father was going to be a big actor. My mother wanted to be a singer.

"She had a good voice. For a while, she sang for the National Conservatory. But, because of the way things were in those times, that didn't last.

"For a while, she survived by giving singing lessons at home. Then, she sang in the concentration camp in Terezin. She said that that was good.

"The good thing about Terezin (which was probably the best of the concentration camps) was the Nazis would always show off Terezin to the concerned people from neutral countries like Switzerland, or from the Red Cross.

"But just because Terezin was better than all the other camps, it still wasn't so good. You never knew when it was going to be your turn to be transported to the other camps, which were always worse, and you never heard from people after that.

"Most of my family went to Terezin first before they were transported to the other camps. I tried to find out what happened to them, but all that information was lost, and doesn't exist, and I never did find out what happened to them."

Then, Hanne shared a part of her experience that startled me - the revelation that her mother had survived the Holocaust, and been liberated from the Terezin concentration camp.

"When we finally located my mother," Hanne said, "she was in Vienna. From there, my aunt and uncle made arrangements for her to join us.

"When we met her at the train station, I could still tell that she was my mother, but she didn't look the same. She was obviously quite ill and emaciated.

"For a year, she lived with us; but it was complicated. I think that my mother understood that my aunt and uncle had saved my life. The children and the old people in the camps were always the first to go, and if I had been there with my mother, I wouldn't have made it.

"Still, it was difficult for my mother, because I think that she also felt my aunt and uncle had supplanted her role with me.

"My aunt tried to be good to my mother, and help her get over what had happened to her at the camp.

"But, also, there were times that my aunt felt my mother needed to make changes, and didn't want to baby her.

"Finally, the two of them had a big blowout, and my mother left the house and went into the village.

"There, my mother became ill, and it wasn't long before she was admitted to the hospital, and then died."

To be continued.

Postscript:

Later, family members confided that Hanne's mother went to the hospital because of an attempted suicide that was ultimately successful.

CHAPTER TWENTY

Part 6 concludes Hanne's story with her new life in United States.
Michael Yanuck
Waxing Philosophical
The Paris Post-Intelligencer, Paris, Tenn., Page 2, February 5th, 2010.

Just before going to press with the final installment of Hanne's story, I visited Hanne. The wound on her leg was still slow to heal, and her doctor had made an appointment for her with a surgeon.
"Hopefully, he won't cut it off," she joked.
She said that she had read my book, "Ethel's Story."
"You are a good writer," she said. "Or, at least, I think so. Have you been writing anything lately?"
When I told her that I'd been working on a story about her, she responded, "You shouldn't write anything about me. I'm no hero. I am an anti-hero."
Naturally, I would beg to differ, and try to convey this point in this the finale of Hanne's story.

Hanne, who survived the Holocaust as a hidden child, surprised me with the revelation that her mother had survived World War II and her internment in a concentration camp.

This, too, however, would be punctuated with poignancy, as her mother died within a year of her reunion with Hanne.

"I don't know exactly what I felt then," Hanne said. "I think that I was confused. I had known so many people who had died.

"The truth is, I think that my saddest day in the whole war was in the beginning when they sent my (maternal) grandparents to the camps.

"Before then, my grandfather had been the center of my world. He would take me on walks everyday. When the family would get together, he would always take out his fiddle and play.

"He and my grandmother were sent to the camps in 1942 and, even back then, we knew what was happening.

"Some of the things we heard were so terrible that you didn't believe them. People gassed. People starved.

"Most of this information came from the underground, so you couldn't be sure that it was reliable. In the end, though, it all turned out to be true."

Hanne paused, and I looked about the hospital room, at a loss for words.

Just then, a nurse came through the doorway, and announced that Hanne was being discharged.

"All the blood work came back normal," the nurse said. "The doctor will call in some antibiotics to your pharmacy. You're free to go home."

We helped Hanne into her wheelchair, and then took her to the car.

On the road, I asked Hanne how the Holocaust experience had affected her view of life.

"It makes life different," she said. "Most people, when they think about their childhood memories, I think that they have happy thoughts of the past. They go back to those thoughts when they grew older, and it gives them comfort.

"But my thoughts are not so happy. So I don't think that I will be like a lot of people. Instead, I take life day by day, and just see what happens."

Not far from Hanne's home, we passed a restaurant called "The Mill," about which I had heard good things.

"I have never been there," Hanne said.

"But it's right across the way from your home," I responded. "Come on, we'll all go now."

I swung the car around, and turned back for the restaurant. But the night was cold and rainy, and it was impossible to traverse the walkway with Hanne's wheelchair, because there were so many steps.

Hanne's walking was unsteady, and I was afraid that at any moment she might fall. "What are you doing?" I asked myself. "Hanne's just been released from the hospital. You should take her home."

Then, a passing couple took an interest, and offered to assist us with Hanne.

"I used to do this for a living," the woman said. Then, she turned to Hanne. "Here, take my arms and we'll get down those last steps."

Inside, the hostess seated us next to the fireplace. Peering through the window, Hanne looked out at the running water that used to power the mill.

"I think that maybe I did come to this restaurant before," Hanne said. "Once with Gil."

Gil was Hanne's now-deceased husband.

"How did you meet Gil?" I asked.

"It was after college," Hanne said. "I was in New York working as an accountant. Gil was working as an accountant, too. We worked in the same office, but when he asked me if I wanted to go out with him, I was too nervous to tell him yes.

"Then, Gil's mother, who also worked in the office, told me that Gil was a good person. She was a middle-aged woman, and, because of that, I thought that what she would be telling me was all right.

"So, the next time Gil asked me, I said yes." Hanne hesitated, and appeared in deep reflection.

I'd been told that Hanne's aunt and uncle had opposed her relationship with Gil, on the basis that he was Puerto Rican, and somehow "beneath her." When the aunt and uncle insisted that Hanne stop seeing Gil, Hanne and Gil eloped.

But before I could ask about this, Hanne smiled, then leaned forward on the table, and looked me straight in the eye.

"So there!" Hanne declared. "It was all her (Gil's mother's) fault!"

I laughed, and Hanne seized the moment.

"It's much too nice a place to keep talking about such things," she said. "Time to talk about something else."

"Wait," I thought. "We're not finished. There's still a story to be told.

"Hanne, you're the product of the Holocaust's two principle antagonists - part-German, part-Jew - conceived at a time of one of the worst and most horrific struggles in human history, who then goes on to marry a man completely outside your faith and experience?

"Don't you see? Yours is a testament to love. And your story should be shared with every grade-school child in the country."

But Hanne just returned to a lively discussion, laughing and smiling and thoroughly enjoying her meal.

So, dear reader, it appears that I've done as much as I can do.

And how Hanne's story will resonate into the future? That it seems is left to you.

Postscript:

It is sometimes funny how one story can weave into another.

Shortly after Hanne told me that she didn't consider herself a hero, I was interviewed for a position with the Indian Health Service. The person interviewing me was Native American (Lakota Sioux) who had an intense interest in the Holocaust and renown Holocaust survivors like Elie Wiesel.

"I heard Elie Wiesel speak once," he said. "He told people, 'I am not a hero. I survived. I would eat my grandmother's bread if I could.

"'The hero's are the ones who gave of their bread. They were the heroes.' And you know what happened to them - most of them did not survive..."

CHAPTER TWENTY-ONE

Anne Frank changed the world.
Michael Yanuck
Waxing Philosophical
The Paris Post-Intelligencer, Paris, Tenn., Page 2, April 9, 2010.

My beloved mother-in-law never talks about seizing the day, she simply does it in every moment.
And in her whirlwind of never ending possibilities and adventure, I usually can't help but be swept along.
This was the case when she introduced me to Ms. Ruth Klemens, who knew Anne Frank.

Who would ever think that so much went on in the soul of a young girl?
~Anne Frank, 1929-1945.

Entering the sanctuary for Shabbat services, my friend's mother pulls me aside and says that there's someone who she'd like me to meet.

"Her name is Ruth Klemens," she says. "She knew Anne Frank."

"The Anne Frank?!" I respond.

"Yes, Ruth grew up with Anne Frank in Amsterdam," she says. "Then, she saw her again in the concentration camp, Bergen-Belsen. The reason why Ruth survived - and Anne didn't - was because Ruth was part of an exchange program that got her out of the camp. Otherwise, she would have wound up like Anne Frank did."

I'd read the Diary of Anne Frank when I was ten years old, and could have never imagined meeting someone who knew her.

Even then, Anne's writing seemed like a time long ago in distant history; so the thought that now, almost forty years later, I was about to meet someone who was connected with Anne Frank was hard for me to grasp.

"I really don't know what exactly it is you want to learn from me," Ruth said upon my being introduced. "I was born in Germany in 1927, but in 1933 my father saw what was coming, and he made plans for all of us to leave Germany, and in 1934 we did.

"But we didn't go very far. We went to the Netherlands. That was wonderful. The Dutch were a very well disposed nation towards Jews, towards immigrants, towards refugees. They took in a lot of people. But they lived with the false hope that there would be no invasion, that they would be saved like they were during World War I, when they were left neutral. But this was not to be.

"We lived in Amsterdam, and life there was very pleasant. We joined a temple with members from other German Jewish communities. That's how I knew Anne Frank.

"I was never best friends with Anne. Anne was a little younger, and in those days, somebody who was younger you didn't like to associate with. I thought Anne was flighty, and always silly to me. Anne's older sister, Margot, was somebody who I really admired, because she was a serious young girl, and very studious."

As I've told you, what I say is not what I feel, which is why I have a reputation for being boy-crazy as well as a flirt, a smart aleck and a reader of romances. The happy-go-lucky Anne laughs, gives a flippant reply, shrugs her shoulders and pretends she doesn't give a darn. The quiet Anne reacts in just the opposite way. - The Diary of Anne Frank.

"My father went to America, where he tried to get us out," Ruth continued. "But he couldn't get the permits in time.

"My mother was with us, and she tried anything she could. My father was a German World War I veteran, and had letters of distinction and medals that my mother would try to use to keep us out of the camps. When the Germans would come to take us, my mother would show them the Iron Crosses, and say, 'Look at what my husband did. These are his children. Can't you do something?' But they didn't.

"And then you paid a large sum of money so that you wouldn't be sent off, but that didn't work either.

"That was the way it was: We were Jewish, and when the Germans entered Holland, the first thing they did was have all the Jews wear an ID card with the letter 'J' on it.

"How did they know who was Jewish? Well, also the Dutch had a list of people belonging here and there. You were innocently giving this information at one point, not thinking that it would be used against you in any way. But it was.

"I was first sent to the Westerbork camp in the Netherlands. It was cold in the camp, and there was no form of heating. I had just turned 16, so I had to work. We all had to harvest potatoes. It was pretty tough work, and we were all given these wooden shoes because the ground was full of clay, and you would sink right into it. That's why the Dutch farmers wore the wood shoes before it became a fashion statement.

"After the harvest, I was assigned to the camp laundry, and I worked there until the time that I was sent to Bergen-Belsen concentration camp in Germany.

"Then, when I was in Bergen-Belsen towards the end of 1944, there was a big transfer that came from the East, and there were rumors that they had Dutch people among them. That's when Anne and her sister came from Auschwitz.

"We weren't allowed to communicate; we weren't allowed to even look at them through the fence. But we did.

"They had these sheet-like garments. That was late December and it was really cold. Not that we had such warm things, but they had absolutely nothing. They had these sheets that they wore, because all of their clothes had either rotted away or been taken away.

"I had a little notebook that I carried in my pocket, and used as a diary to write down events. That's where I wrote that I had seen Anne and Margot Frank behind the fence."

(To be continued.)

"Diary of Anne Frank" will be aired by Masterpiece Theater on PBS television stations at 8 p.m. this Sunday. Dr. Michael Yanuck is the former medical director of Stewart County Community Medical Center in Dover. His e-mail address is myanuck@hotmail.com.

Postscript: I actually didn't get to see the Anne Frank production, as I was caring for a beloved Uncle whose health took a sudden turn for the worse. More about that another time.

CHAPTER TWENTY-TWO

Ruth Klemens' mother was a hero, saving her daughters.
Michael Yanuck
Waxing Philosophical
The Paris Post-Intelligencer, Paris, Tenn., Page 2, April 16th, 2010.

On a Friday evening, I was introduced to Ruth Klemens, an older woman who grew up with Anne Frank in Amsterdam.

To Ruth, Anne was a flighty little girl who lived in her neighborhood. Later, their paths would cross again - this time in the Bergen-Belsen concentration camp.

"Bergen-Belsen was a big camp, and it was divided into sections and separated by fences. They had a camp that was for German convicts. They had a camp for gypsies.

"And then, when this Auschwitz group came - that had Anne and her sister - that was another camp. And they didn't have enough space anymore, so what they did was erect a fence near us, and took half our barracks away, and made us all triple-up in the barracks, because we had a new camp for all these people from Auschwitz.

"I noticed Anne and her sister, but I couldn't speak to them. It was forbidden to even try.

"And these people who had come from Auschwitz, they had just little shirts. That was late December, and it was really cold. So the fact that so many of them died there was not unusual to hear after the war.

"We were very fortunate, my mother, sisters and I. We were in the Austauschlager, the 'exchange camp,' where we were intended to be exchanged against German prisoners-of-war.

"We were in this group because my father, who was in America by this time, managed to buy passports for us to Paraguay. People who had Latin American passports were put into the exchange group.

"The Germans treated us better than the others. They didn't want to put [tattooed] numbers on us because, if one day we might get exchanged, they didn't want the outside world to see how we were treated.

"Still, when you came to the camp, the first thing they did was let us have a shower. And of course the word 'shower' was awful, but you couldn't say, 'No, I'm not going in there.'

"Later, when I became a teacher, the school kids would ask me, 'Well, why didn't you just run away? Why did you put up with that?'

"I tell them, 'Well, we didn't have a choice. If you ran, there was no place to run, except the fence. And if you ran to the fence, it was electrified. Some people still did run - some in desperation, others I don't know why.'

"There was only one exchange for prisoners of war, and it was only 60 or 70 people who were involved.

"We were fortunate for being all women - my mother, sisters and me. For obvious reasons, they didn't want to send any eligible young men who could fight. So, we had that advantage.

"But you could never be sure that you were free until you were out of their clutches. Many of the German prisoners of war changed their minds, and decided that they didn't want to be in the exchange, because they knew the end of the war was coming, and didn't want to be in Germany then.

"Since the exchange had to be one-for-one, many in our exchange group had to stay behind.

"My mother was very ill, and I knew she would have died in the camp if we were sent back. She was thin as a rail. She never ate anything. I think now that she must have given us every bit of food she had.

"She had no stamina, and when the German came to interview us to see if we ready to go on the trip to be exchanged, she looked so weak.

"But when they asked her, she said, 'I'm ready.' And she was - she walked with us and everything.

"Later, a German soldier saw how sick my mother was, and tried to pull us off the train. But she stood straight, and said that she was fine and, after a while, he left us alone.

"After the exchange, my mother did die upon our arrival in Switzerland.

"Two or three people were buried in the same place that my mother was. At the cemetery, they had a special monument erected. It said, 'Their strength lasted till they became free.'"

(To be continued.)

Postscript:

Shortly after her mother died, Ruth came upon a regimen of US soldiers. In fact, that night she and her sister were invited to dance.

"I remember thinking, 'One day I was in a concentration camp,'" she said. "'A little after that, my mother died. Now, I was here at this party with a lot of American GI's.' It all seemed so odd."

Life goes on, I thought. And you never know what might happen.

CHAPTER TWENTY-THREE

Anne Frank's diary helped Ruth come to terms with Holocaust.
Michael Yanuck
Waxing Philosophical
The Paris Post-Intelligencer, Paris, Tenn., Page 2, April 23rd, 2010.

In this part of the Anne Frank series, Ruth Klemens describes how it was reading Anne Frank's diary that helped her come to terms with her Holocaust experience. I think it also helped her feel more for the sanctity of life, as she had no inkling of the depth of Anne Frank. And also Ruth found that the Diary made the Holocaust real for her students, so that they wouldn't forget it.

On a Friday evening, I was introduced to Ruth Klemens, an older woman who grew up with Anne Frank during the time of the Holocaust.

To Ruth, Anne was a flighty little girl who lived in her neighborhood. Later, their paths would cross again in the Bergen-Belsen concentration camp.

Ruth survived the Holocaust, mostly because an exchange for German prisoners-of-war permitted her to leave the camp, and be set free.

"After that [the exchange], we were supposed to be taken on a boat to North Africa," she continued. "But my father pulled strings, and my sisters and I were transferred to a Swedish hospital ship to America, where my father was waiting for us.

"When we came to this country, we tried to become a part of American life. My English wasn't the best, and it took time to learn. I was 17 years old then.

"When the other students asked me where I'd been, I wasn't interested in telling them. I just told them that I grew up in Holland. They wanted to know what it was like, and the windmills, and I wouldn't have begun to tell them about what had happened during the war."

Then, Anne Frank's diary was published, and all that changed.

"It was in 1947. A friend of mine had bought the book for me in Holland. She knew that I would be interested, and she gave it to me to read.

"I remember sitting out in her garden, reading the book from cover to cover, and finding it unbelievable that somebody I had known as a flighty young girl a year younger than I was — she was always silly to me — was capable of writing with such feeling and understanding, as she was.

"And I couldn't believe it. If her sister had done it — yes, she was a serious type. But there must have been something there that was touched by what happened — because I was a little thrown for a loop when I read it."

In her diary, Anne Frank wrote, "I look back at that Anne Frank as a pleasant, amusing, but superficial girl, who has nothing to do with me.

"What did Peter say about me? 'Whenever I saw you, you were surrounded by a flock of girls and at least two boys, you were always laughing, and you were always the center of attention!' He was right.

"What's remained of that Anne Frank? Oh, I haven't forgotten to laugh or toss off a remark, I'm just as good, if not better, at raking people over the coals, and I can still flirt and be amusing, if I want to be.

"But there's the catch. I'd like to live that seemingly carefree and happy life for an evening, a few days, a week. At the end of that week, I'd be exhausted, and would be grateful to the first person to talk to me about something meaningful.

"I want friends, not admirers — people who respect me for my character and my deeds, not my flattering smile. The circle around me would be much smaller, but what does that matter, as long as they're sincere?"

"I don't think there was any particular passage that grabbed me more than others," Ruth continued. "Just the whole idea that somebody of that age could be so sensitive to everything, and write so beautifully, and have very mature feelings, too.

"I thought it was marvelous. I thought it was uncanny — the whole thing. I've often picked it up and read passages again, because I find it so hard to make myself understand that she wrote this.

"I was a teacher then, and when I told some of the students who were reading The Diary of Anne Frank that I actually had met her, they couldn't believe it. 'Oh, you're famous,' I remember them saying. 'Can I have your autograph?'

"These were middle school kids, and they had different concepts. But the fact that there was a Holocaust — I don't think they ever forgot that."

To be continued.

Postscript:

During the publication of this series, I watched to documentary, "Jenin, Jenin," a film that captured the plight of the Palestinians – a people who might have lost a battle, but were well on their way to achieving greater and greater levels of awareness, ability and accomplishment, fighting for their rights and homeland.

In the film, the Jenin population sit amongst the rubble, and curse the Israelis who leveled their city. They call the Israelis "inhuman." And I also regard them such, and what they did a blasphemy. A blasphemy before the eyes of god. And a blasphemy to the Jewish race.

Is this where a God of mercy resides? I thought. Is this where a holy people reside? A righteous people? Chosen people?

Then, I seemed to find this generations Anne Frank. She's a little girl, perhaps 10 years old, who sits amongst the remnants of her ruined city and fearlessly stares into the camera, and declares that she will fight the murderer, Ariel Sharon.

Other children where interviewed for the documentary. In general, they smiled, giggle and laughed. But not this child. She never laughed. She simply spoke her truth, without any sign of fear or shame or self-doubt.

A real lioness, I thought. She could not only reach the conscience of the world, but demand appropriate action.

CHAPTER TWENTY-FOUR

Ruth Klemens concludes her recollections of Anne Frank.
Michael Yanuck
Waxing Philosophical
The Paris Post-Intelligencer, Paris, Tenn., Page 2, April 30th, 2010.

On a Friday evening, my mother-in-law introduced me to Ruth Klemens, an older woman who grew up with Anne Frank in Amsterdam.

To Ruth, Anne was just a flighty little girl who lived in her neighborhood. Later, their paths crossed again in the Bergen-Belsen concentration camp.

"In the camp, we were given bread to last us for the week," Ruth said. "I remember, we were given a chunk of three or four pieces, and it had to last you for the week. You had to guard it with your life, because, if you didn't, somebody might get it. Most people put it under their pillow. They slept on it because that was about the safest place at night.

"And bread became also a type of currency, because with all this, there were still people who were addicted to smoking, and if somebody had a cigarette, they would give up their bread gladly. And they did.

"So bread was of the utmost importance. I don't remember anybody sharing their bread, except perhaps my mom, who gave her bread to us.

"Yet, I don't know. Some of it was pretty gruesome. People were really driven to the extreme. Not everybody was strong enough to withstand the temptations."

Anne Frank wrote, "At night in bed, I see myself alone in a dungeon, without Father and Mother. Or I'm roaming the streets, or the Annex is on fire, or they come in the middle of the night to take us away and I crawl under my bed in desperation. I see everything as if it were actually taking place. And to think it might all happen soon!"

It wasn't in the middle of the night, but, rather, about 10 a.m. on Aug. 4, 1944, that a car pulled up at 263 Prinsengracht, and an SS sergeant and three Dutch police officers arrested Anne and the others who had been hiding in the secret Annex.

"I see the eight of us in the Annex, as if we were a patch of blue sky surrounded by menacing black clouds," Anne wrote. "The perfectly round spot on which we're standing is still safe, but the clouds are moving in on us, and the ring between us and the approaching danger is being pulled tighter and tighter.

"We're surrounded by darkness and danger, and in our desperate search for a way out, we keep bumping into each other. We look at the fighting down below and the peace and beauty up above.

"In the meantime, we've been cut off by the dark mass of clouds, so that we can go neither up nor down. It looms before us like an impenetrable wall, trying to crush us, but not yet able to. I can only cry out and implore, 'Oh, ring, ring, open wide and let us out!'"

By all accounts, Anne Frank died a miserable death. Separated from her parents at Auschwitz (where her mother perished), and then, plagued by disease, starvation and exhaustion, Anne endured the Bergen-Belsen concentration camp until that life of hers — that light — was finally snuffed out.

"The Frank girls were so emaciated," a barrack mate said. "They looked terrible. They had hollowed-out faces, skin over bone. They were terribly cold.

"They had the least desirable places in the barracks, below, near the door, which was constantly opened and closed. You heard them constantly scream, 'Close the door, close the door,' and the voices became weaker every day.

"Suddenly, I didn't see them anymore. I didn't pay any special attention to them, because there were so many others who also died there, down there on that bunk."

"I don't believe the war is simply the work of politicians and capitalists," Anne Frank wrote. "Oh no, the common man is every bit as guilty; otherwise, people and nations would have rebelled long ago!

"There's a destructive urge in people, the urge to rage, murder and kill. And until all of humanity, without exception, undergoes a metamorphosis, wars will continue to be waged, and everything that has been carefully built up, cultivated and grown will be cut down and destroyed, only to start all over again!"

Ruth Klemens shook her head, and then talked about her concerns for children and their parents in the present.

"I recently had surgery," she said. "We have good insurance, but you look at the amounts that they're billing the hospital for, and the numbers are simply astronomical. You wonder how all that gets paid?

"What happens to the people who don't have insurance? What do they do when they have to go to the hospital? What kinds of bills do they run up? How will they ever pay for them? Who will take care of them?"

Leaving Ruth, I thought about the challenges in the future, and wondered whose "flighty" little girl might write the words that would again stir the conscience of humanity.

"Everyone has, inside of him, a piece of good news," Anne Frank wrote. "The good news is that you don't know how great you can be! How much you can love! What you can accomplish! And what your potential is!"

Postscript:

I had wanted to conclude the piece by challenging the reader, and to the question of the next "flighty" little girl whose writing might again stir the conscience of the world, asking: "Who knows? Maybe, it will it be your child? Or, perhaps, you'll fight for a better world, so that no child's story will be necessary to awaken our humanity?"

My wise wife, however, felt this was to confrontational.

In the meantime, during the publication of this series, my former girlfriend, Cathy, wrote that she had lost her job with the Paris school system, and was concerned about how she'd support the children..

Given my circumstances at the time, there was little I could do, except hope that out of these hardships, something deeper and more lasting would take hold and bloom.

During the publication of this series, I watched to documentary, "Jenin, Jenin," a great film that captured the plight of the Palestinians – a people who might have lost a battle, but were well on their way to achieving greater and greater levels of awareness, ability and accomplishment, fighting for their rights and homeland.

In the film, the Jenin population sit amongst the rubble, and curse the Israelis who leveled their city. They call the Israelis "inhuman." And I also regard them such, and what they did a blasphemy. A blasphemy before the eyes of god. And a blasphemy to the Jewish race.

Is this where a God of mercy resides? I thought. Is this where a holy people reside? A righteous people? Chosen people?

Then, I seemed to find this generations Anne Frank. She's a little girl, perhaps 10 years old, who sits amongst the remnants of her ruined city and fearlessly stares into the camera, and declares that she will fight the murderer, Ariel Sharon.

Other children where interviewed for the documentary. In general, they smiled, giggle and laughed. But not this child. She never laughed. She simply spoke her truth, without any sign of fear or shame or self-doubt.

A real lioness, I thought. She could not only reach the conscience of the world, but demand appropriate action.

CHAPTER TWENTY-FIVE

Fate of Pincus' mom
Michael Yanuck
Waxing Philosophical
The Paris Post-Intelligencer, Paris, Tenn., Page 2, June 4th, 2010.

I toiled with how to begin the telling of this next piece. I was concerned that I had not provided the readers with adequate context.
Still, I couldn't bring myself to alter my Aunt's description, and hoped that my readers - and you - will simply be as gripped as I was.

Never shall I forget that night, the first night in camp, which has turned my life into one long night, seven times cursed and seven times sealed.
Never shall I forget that smoke. Never shall I forget the little faces of the children, whose bodies I saw turned into wreaths of smoke beneath a silent blue sky.
Never shall I forget those flames which consumed my faith forever.
Never shall I forget that nocturnal silence which deprived me, for all eternity, of the desire to live.
Never shall I forget those moments which murdered my God and my soul and turned my dreams to dust.
Never shall I forget these things, even if I am condemned to live as long as God Himself. Never.
—Elie Wiesel, Night

A few weeks ago I described the events of my uncle's passing.

On the occasion of his funeral, among the family members who I visited with was my aunt.

My uncle and she had actually divorced some years earlier, and she had remarried a Holocaust survivor named Pincus Kolender.

Pincus was born in 1926 in Bochnia, Poland. At the age of 16, he went to Auschwitz. After World War II, he settled in South Carolina, where he ultimately became widely known for sharing his Holocaust experiences.

During their marriage, my aunt attended his every speaking engagement, and considered herself his greatest fan. Sadly, though, Pincus, like my uncle, had also recently passed away.

Now, greeting me at the door, my aunt appeared bereaved. Although I was excited to see her again, I wondered if she felt the same. After all, it had been many years, and really, since my uncle and she had divorced, it could be said that she was no longer my aunt.

But she was willing to sit and talk, and imparted many of the Holocaust experiences of her recently deceased husband, Pincus.

Perhaps the most moving of these experiences was about the fate of Pincus' mother. I title this, "On the nightmare of a Holocaust victim."

"Whenever Pincus would give a talk and they would ask about how his mother died," my Aunt began, "I knew there was going to be a nightmare that night.

"It wasn't the first roundup, because Pincus' grandmother and sister had already been sent to Belzec [a concentration camp in Poland].

"But this was one of the times when the Germans had given a directive to the president of the Judenrat [Jewish council overseeing the ghetto] that he was to ship out all but 150. They wanted only 150 left in the ghetto.

"And of course this one went to the president, and that one went to him. Pincus' father was a good friend of his, and said, 'Please put us on the list [of those who would remain in the ghetto, and not be transported to the concentration camp],' as did all these other people.

"So when the commandant came and lined everybody up, he said, 'This is too many. You were told to leave 150, and this is more than 150.'

"So they counted, and it was somewhere's over 200. They were standing in family groups, so the commandant just went down the line, and said, 'You and you and you and you.'

"One of the 'yous' was Pincus' mother. They had been standing father, mother, Pincus and his brother — standing together. He picked out his mother.

"So they put them to a wall, had them face the wall — mowed them all down.

"Then, the commandant called on some of the boys — 'You, you and you' — to take the bodies and stack them up. Then, they would pour gasoline on them and light the fire. One of the boys was Pincus.

"Now, Pincus' mother was kind of on the end of one of the aisles, and this was at dusk also. So Pincus pulled her body away and put it over by the wall, thinking that maybe no one would notice, and he could give her a decent burial the next day.

"Well, one of the soldiers saw him, and said, 'You God d--- Jew. Go put that body back with the others.'"

To be continued.

Postscript:

The reception that I received from my Aunt did seem rather chilly. Naturally, I didn't really know the details of her life with my late Uncle; my wife thought that problem of bipolar disorder that runs in my family might have been part of it, and left her life significantly scarred.

The divorce from my deceased Uncle was said to be unpleasant, and further soured by the fact that my brother (who she'd had a hand in raising for a year in Missouri) had initially acted as my Uncle's attorney in those proceedings.

It did get better, though, and, for that, I have mostly Pincus to thank.

CHAPTER TWENTY-SIX

Burning mother's body worsened Pincus' nightmares.
Michael Yanuck
Waxing Philosophical
The Paris Post-Intelligencer, Paris, Tenn., Page 2, June 18th, 2010.

"... (T)o remain silent and indifferent is the greatest sin of all ..."
— *Elie Wiesel.*

On the occasion of my uncle's funeral, another relative and I visited with his ex-wife, my aunt. Many years had passed since I'd last seen her, and much had happened in the interim.

She and my uncle had divorced, so that, technically, she was no longer my aunt, and I wondered if she was really all that interested in seeing me again.

Additionally, she'd remarried to a Holocaust survivor named Pincus Kolender, who she greatly admired and, like my uncle, had recently passed away.

Before his death, Pincus had toured his adopted state of South Carolina, sharing his Holocaust experience. My aunt had accompanied him everywhere he spoke, and could re-tell his stories verbatim.

Of the stories she shared, the most poignant related to the death of Pincus' mother, who had been executed in front of him before the Nazis gave him the task of collecting her body and burning it.

Much to his peril, Pincus had tried to hide his mother's body, so he could give her a decent burial; however, he was caught by a German soldier.

What follows is the conclusion of that story, as told by my aunt:

"'You God d--- Jew,' [the German soldier told Pincus]. 'Go put that body back with the others.' And then the soldier hit Pincus with the butt of the rifle.

"So Pincus did. He moved his mother's body back over, and poured the gasoline on and lighted the fire.

"That night — and this all took place just outside the wall of the ghetto — he and a friend sneaked out, and he had a can with him, and he thought he knew approximately where her body was.

"So he scraped up the ashes from that place, put them in the can and then took them to a tree near there and buried them — thinking that, if and when he was able to come back, he would give her a decent burial.

"Well, [years later] the first time they went back — it was Pincus and one of his children and his wife and some cousins — several of them had shovels, and they were digging here and there.

"But the fence was gone that had been there. And the tree was gone that had been there. So they used poles and went down into the earth, and they did everything trying to find it [the can with his mother's remains]. But they weren't able to find it, so he just said prayers then and there.

"Pincus was not quite 14 years old when it happened," my aunt concluded. "Things like that, they were so unnecessary, and then they all had to stand and watch."

I told her about my recent interview with another Holocaust victim, Ruth Klemens, who had known Anne Frank, and who had lost her mother shortly after being set free from the Bergen-Belsen concentration camp.

"Within a week of her mother's passing," I said, "Ruth was invited by some American soldiers to a dance. Later, she remembered thinking, 'How was it that I could have been enjoying life at a time like that? How does life go on?'"

"It does," my aunt said, grimly. She reflected for a moment.

"Pincus said that he doesn't remember specifically meeting Elie Wiesel [Holocaust victim, writer and recipient of the Nobel Peace Prize]," she continued.

"People would ask him, because he was in that same camp as Wiesel. Pincus said, 'You didn't care to know anybody. You didn't know anybody's last name, and you didn't really want to know.'

"But, since that time, he's had occasion to be introduced to Elie Wiesel. A couple of years ago, Elie Wiesel was in Columbia in South Carolina to give a speech there, and we made arrangements to go to Columbia for it.

"When we got there, we looked for our table cards and I said, 'That's strange. We're not sitting at the same table.' That's very unusual to go to something where there's 200 or 300 people and they've separated couples.

"Pincus said, 'Well, there's got to be a mistake.' First, we went to the cocktail reception, and Wiesel was there, and he remembered Pincus from the last time they were at a speaking engagement together.

"Then, we went to where the reception was, and we figured out why we weren't sitting together. I was seated at the table with the wife of the president of the college and several other dignitaries. Pincus is seated not only at the table with Elie Wiesel — he was sitting next to Elie Wiesel.

"And he said — and this was typical Pincus — 'Why me? Why not somebody else?' He just could not get it, that anybody was giving him accolades."

"But he paid for that," another relative said. "He felt like he needed to do that, talk about his experience. He would have nightmares. It played on his mind."

"It was just part of who he was," my aunt said. "It was part of his makeup."

"Not only that," my relative said, "but the fact that he survived. And the fact that he continued on."

My aunt smiled. "Like he said," she imparted, "he was 'too stubborn to die.'"

"And he was generous," my relative added, "talking to people."

"Generous and giving of himself," my aunt affirmed.

"And when you go through something like that," my relative said, "something so horrible. And you realize that there are people out there who not only don't ... [care], but will do you in. Well, how do you not hate? How don't you get cold yourself?

"And here you have a person who not only went through all of that, but remained generous. I mean, how do you not honor that?"

I said Pincus' example might have been a lesson to people.

My aunt nodded. "He taught them how to be a human being," she said.

Then, for the first time, my aunt's features lightened, and she smiled.

"Would you all like something to drink?" she asked. "I've been sitting here all this time, not offering you anything ...."

Postscript:
And so - even dead and buried - it seemed that Pincus had a

significant hand in resurrecting my relationship with my Aunt.

In the Jewish tradition, there are stories that the dead walk the earth out of concerned for those they've left behind. After our visit with my Aunt, I thought that Pincus had a little less to be worried about.

May we all have such an kindly influence on those we love and hold dear.

CHAPTER TWENTY-SEVEN

Israel must banish discrimination.
Michael Yanuck
Waxing Philosophical
The Paris Post-Intelligencer, Paris, Tenn., Page 2, October 22, 2008.

William Barr's Oct. 2 column, "Israel condemns 'hooligans,' and yet encourages them," gave me cause for reflection.

Previously, in my Sept. 25 "Understanding race" submission, I wrote about how I discovered what it felt like to be among the "majority" while living in Israel.

But, at the same time, I saw things that were difficult to witness, and left me at a loss.

My first such encounter happened when I missed the last bus traveling north to the coastal city of Haifa.

A cab driver saw me walking away despondent, and asked if he could give me a ride. I told him that I didn't have much money.

"That's OK," he said. "We find someone to share the fare with you."

An older woman agreed to share the fare, and we drove off together.

"Where are you going?" the woman asked me.

Haifa, I told her.

"Not good," she said. "That's a long way. You should get off with me at Tel Aviv, and then take another cab. This driver is Arab."

Glancing in the driver's direction, I felt certain that he'd overheard the woman, and could only imagine what he was feeling.

Not long after, while camping along the Sea of Galilee, I awoke to find a tent next to ours. Along the shore a group of "Israeli Arab" young men were playing soccer, and my traveling companions and I joined them.

Afterwards, the Arab men invited us to share breakfast with them. Though my friends and I brought out all of our food supplies, our contribution was meager compared to theirs.

Still, the Arab men took no offense, and greeted us with only smiles. I don't think that I've ever partaken of watermelon so sweet.

Then, shortly after this encounter, I saw something that has remained etched in my consciousness ever since.

While visiting the burial grounds of the Hebrew forefathers in Hebron, my traveling companions and I got lost, and wound up in a Palestinian refugee camp in the then-occupied West Bank.

Within the camp, the people sat baking in the hot desert sun; it was as though they were trapped there like cattle, with no place to go.

Yet, in their faces, there was a look of resolve, as though they would stay there for however long it took, and wait until the day when they could return to their former lands within the boundaries of Israel.

Some Israelis have told me that Americans have no place reserving judgment on their policies towards the Israeli Arabs and Palestinians.

"Look at the way that you Americans treated the Indians," one said. "And then, the war you fought with Mexico to take away their land. Are you going to give it back now?"

At the same time, however, many Israelis express weariness for further fighting.

"More and more Israeli young men are trying to get out of their required three-year service in the Army," an Israeli told me. "It's like the entire population of Israel is suffering from Post-Traumatic Stress Disorder."

Sunday, I traveled into Washington, D.C., again, and walked along the FDR Memorial Park. Among the eloquent quotes from President Roosevelt inscribed in the memorial's walls is this one:

"We must scrupulously guard the civil rights and civil liberties of all our citizens, whatever their background. We must remember that any oppression, any injustice, any hatred, is a wedge designed to attack our civilization."

Afterwards, I crossed Independence Avenue, turned on 14th Street and meandered into the Holocaust Museum.

There, while standing before a photograph of a Nazi soldier brutally kicking one of my soon-to-be-exterminated brethren into the cattle car of a train bound for the death camps, something occurred to me:

The Holocaust was born mostly out of discrimination; and from the Nazi atrocities, the state of Israel was formed. And now it's time that Israel banish all remnants of discrimination from its society, so that peoples of all faiths and races can live there in peace.

Postscript:

A story I never wound sharing in many ways follows from how that Arab cabdriver was treated.

I'm going to share it with you here:

Gaza Boy at the Sea of Galilee

The adventure began when Ati introduced us to her new friend, a pudgy Russian Jewish fella who owned a car.

Ati was an attractive, fun, gregarious, German summer student woman, who'd been out with Georg and me before. She was outgoing, friendly, curious, and invited George and I to travel with she and the Russian to the Sea of Galilee for the weekend.

The trip started out on a questionable note, when we discovered the shore was teaming with clams; yet, when we asked several Israeli passersby if they were safe to eat, all offered conflicting opinions: "Yes, they're delicious", or, "No, you don't eat that", and each was so definite in his or her opinion that it left me scratching my head.

"How could this be?" I asked, turning to the others, exasperated.

In response, our Russian escort smiled, knowingly.

"The ones who say not to eat them are religious," he explained. "Shellfish are not kosher…"

Setting up a tent not far from the shore, we brought out a soccer ball, and George invited some of young men in the next tent over to play with us.

They were four fellas about my size and age. None spoke English or Hebrew, but they were keen to play with us. One of them was a very handsome, serious fella with a similar thin, slender build as mine and who played the sport intensely. I felt no qualms about mixing it up with him, and engaged he and the others with competitive fervor. But Georg got overwhelmed when they charged him all at once, and went down smiling (with that handsome, mature, good-natured laugh of his) and asked for a break?

Returning to our tents, Georg and I brought out some of our food to share to share with them; they, in turn, brought out even more, so that we wound up partaking in quite a feast (I remember their tasty, fresh watermelon best).

Then, it happened that the handsome, athletic fella with my similar build appeared to take a spontaneously liking to me. Smiling, he put his arm around my shoulder, then led me around by the hand.

I figured he was just being friendly, and it was a cultural thing that I could accept without judgment.

It was 'Eastern', I told myself. 'Oriental' was the way I thought Edward Syed described it. 'Cultural.'

And I was happy to avail myself up to his culture: I liked that there was friendliness and warmth and closeness between men in his culture; that they were welcoming, and this was the way they treated others. I did not particularly like the masculine, testosterone-driven male culture that I came from, and given how left out I usually felt, I found his conduct pleasant and, indeed, flattering.

He spoke, but I didn't understand him. It turned out, though, that as well as English and Hebrew, the Russian fellow was also fluent in Arabic and translated, saying that he was inviting me to come and spend time with him near the beach where he lived in Gaza; that his uncle owned a boat, and we could go out sailing. Looking back at the young man and his friends, they nodded.

The young man invited me to take a walk along the shore; but I responded that I wanted to stay with my friends, mostly because I was shy.

The next thing I knew, though, it seemed the young man fell into some odd despair; appearing as though devastated (like he'd been hit by a proverbial truck); and so overwhelmed that his friends had to support him, as they consoled him and led him away.

Looking on, I couldn't be sure of what had transpired, and never inquired with anyone about it. I guess I'd just unintentionally committed some faux pas as pertains to his culture? One of those cultural mores that I didn't understand?

Thinking about who I was with respect to him, I regarded myself as just some American guy, spending the summer in Israel, studying cancer research, intent on returning to the United States to become a doctor and a scientist. There wasn't any future for him in my life that I could fathom; we couldn't even individually converse with one another.

But the grief-stricken expression on his face stayed with me: He liked me. His expression of warmth and interest and friendship and reaching out was genuine.

And I think, in part, it fueled an ambition that dictated that when my life in the States was done and my working years were over,

I'd return to Israel to spend my final days there (Back in the place where I'd felt the greatest ease).

And then I'd do what I had always done throughout my medical career, and make my way to helping those in greatest need, which would no doubt take me to the West Bank and Gaza.

I imagined that a violent death awaited me; but it wouldn't matter, because I'd be ready, especially given what I'd seen (like the treatment handed out to the 'Arab' cabdriver).

And in between, maybe I'd have the good fortune of finding others like the young man I'd met from Gaza; who treated me with genuine warmth and kindness; and perhaps I'd get lucky and know some of that again...

CHAPTER TWENTY-EIGHT

My beloved nation of Israel should be beacon of tolerance
Michael Yanuck
Waxing Philosophical
The Paris Post-Intelligencer, Paris, Tenn., Page 2, June 11th, 2010.

   When the following editorial appeared in the paper, I had been between parts one and two of my Pincus Koledar story; however, I interrupted that series, so that I could comment on David Shankle's submission, "Israel attacks flotilla; we look away."

To the editor: When Israeli Defense Forces raided a humanitarian aid flotilla in international waters earlier this week, Israel was condemned, not only by enemies, but also allies alike. There were at least nine civilians killed by Israeli gunfire and dozens more injured. Israeli diplomats immediately cited needs to protect itself against hostilities and weaponry being delivered to Gaza. This propaganda was sold despite the fact that these vessels were not transporting terrorists. They were citizens from Sweden, Australia, Great Britain and even the United States. The flotilla shipped with approval of Turkey, one of Israel's greatest and only Arab allies. They were journalists, former European ambassadors and humanitarian workers revered by champions of peace, such as Archbishop Desmond Tutu. Israel knew about this flotilla weeks in advance, and it was known from the very beginning that there were no weapons being transported on this shipment. In direct violation of the Geneva Convention, it has even blocked the vast majority of attempted humanitarian aid, an international war crime. To add to their repertoire of war crimes, the flotilla that was attacked by Israeli forces never entered Israeli territory. It was attacked in international waters, an act consistently described by the U.N. as blatant piracy. Sadly, this is not news.

By DAVID SHANKLE

Paris Post-Intelligencer

Friday, June 4, 2010

Shankle's letter about Israel's boarding of the Free Gaza flotilla ship, Mavi Marmara, struck a chord in me. Many say that the Holocaust showed that you have to fight for your survival; however, in the present, it's a time to strive for a larger cause.

Not long ago, some Israeli acquaintances had invited me to watch the Academy Award-nominated film from Israel, "Waltz with Bashir." It was an animated documentary about the impact of Israel's 1980 invasion of Lebanon.

In particular, it dealt with how the mass murder of Palestinians by Lebanese Phalangist fighters at the Sabra and Shatila refugee camps affected a number of Israeli soldiers, who had significant reason to suspect that their government was complicit in the massacre.

At the film's end, I sat for a long time looking at the blank screen. When I finally spoke, the only word that I could find to mutter was "Atsov," which in Hebrew means "sad."

"My father had to fight in the war in Lebanon," an Israeli friend said. "He hardly ever talks about what he saw there, except to say that they were firing at everything that moved.

"I think that war was the beginning of the end," she continued. "Shortly after the fighting ended in Lebanon, our family left Israel."

Later, I spoke to my friend's father.

"I entered the war as a medic," he said. "I thought that I could do the most good that way, and really didn't feel comfortable shooting anyone."

The kibbutz [community] where he had lived was situated in the northern part of Israel, just 5 miles from Lebanon border.

Before the Lebanon War, he and his children were continuously evacuated into bomb shelters because of Katyusha rockets launched in their direction by Palestinian fighters.

Scrambling for a shelter during an air raid, one of his children actually saw such a rocket pass right over her head.

"But I was stationed with a lot of right-wingers," he continued.

"At the kibbutz, we were all left-wingers, I guess you'd say — we were all peace-oriented.

"In this unit, the people were speaking in very racist terms. It left me asking myself, 'Are these really my people?'

"That was really the motivation that led me to leave Israel," he concluded.

The war in Lebanon affected me, too.

It was my feeling that Israel was born out of the intolerance that marked the Holocaust, and should, therefore, stand as a beacon of tolerance, willing to endure any hardship to maintain that standard.

I thought that Israel's invasion of Lebanon violated that ideal and, in expressing this view, a number of my meaningful relationships — involving teachers and friends — were strained.

Ultimately, I endeavored to distance myself from my religion.

Oddly, though, at this university where I chose to study, I came under the tutelage of a professor who was an Israeli enthusiast, and whose influence would lead me to travel to Israel and work at the Weizmann Institute of Science in Rehovot, 20 miles south of Tel Aviv.

During that year in Israel, I traveled widely. For a small country, Israel is remarkably diverse geographically.

More than that, by traveling in Israel, I was getting in touch with my roots. Before going there, I treated the Bible as no better than a string of fairy tales meant to convey a moral message.

In Israel, though, I was walking the same ground as my ancestors. In the oasis, Ein Gedi, I probably drank from the same spring as my distant relative, David. In Jerusalem, I walked the Via Dolorosa. My faith had come alive.

But for all my love of the land, I could never come to terms with the hardships faced by the Palestinians and Israeli Arabs.

Now, in the wake of the recent flotilla tragedy, I find myself experiencing the same unsettling feeling as I did when I left Israel; when I purchased a $35 ticket to board a cargo ship bound for Greece - a ship probably not unlike the Mavi Marmara; and, looking out from the stern as the ship departed, I watched the night lights emanating from the port of Haifa become smaller and smaller, until I could see my beloved Israel no longer.

Postscript:

The Free Gaza flotilla conflict struck close to home. At the time, my wife had been planning to go to Turkey to partake in an archaelogical dig. But being that she was Israeli and the majority of those killed by the Israeli raid on the Mavi Marmara had been Turks, the trip had the potential of putting her in danger.

Before submitting this piece, I had written to David Shankle, saying that I appreciated his editorial. He thanked me for the encouragement, saying, "As a member of the military, my views aren't popular. But I still think peace is much more readily welcomed with an extended hand rather than the barrel of a gun and collective punishment."

When he concluded his letter by informing me that "there is currently another flotilla on the way as we speak," my first thought was, "God help us."

After the publication of my article, David wrote to me again.

"Dr. Yanuck, I just wanted to commend you on your latest column," he wrote. "Where my letter was primarily fueled by anger in the wake of those events, perhaps your angle of genuine sympathy is more effective. Your past seems to have informed your current sympathies a great deal. What can I say, after the waves of hate-mail in the past week, I'm just glad to see someone agree with me on some level."

I told David that although I, too, had been the recipient of hate-mail, I was surprised that he'd received any such comments as I hadn't garnered any sense of anger expressed in his submission, and thought it was only an objectively written piece about an issue of significant importance.

"By the way," David added. "I've been fairly interested in learning Hebrew for quite some time. If you'd happen to know of a good resource in those studies, in the way of a good teacher, I'd appreciate it. In searching, none of the local colleges offer anything in the way of foreign languages. Thanks again, David Shankle."

It would have been my pleasure to teach Hebrew to David; however, my travels had taken me quite far from Paris by this time, though my travails were leaving me sorely missing it.

CHAPTER TWENTY-NINE

Do you hear what I hear?
Michael Yanuck
Waxing Philosophical
The Paris Post-Intelligencer, Paris, Tenn., Page 2, December 11, 2007

Living in the small, southern, predominantly Christian town of Paris,
Tennessee exposed me to many new experiences and activities that
gave me a lot of joy. Among them was karaoke...

Sometimes I find it difficult to be Jewish during this time of year.
I enjoy karaoke at The Smokie Doghouse restaurant on Thursday
evenings. But this is the month to sing Christmas songs.

I know all the Christmas songs, and have enjoyed them from
childhood onwards. But, being Jewish, it's difficult to partake in the
reverie. Shouldn't I be singing about Hanukah and dreidels?

What's the Jewish guy doing singing Christmas-carols? Even
when I try to find my own meaning in the music, there's still that
little difference of mine that comes to the fore.

It even finds its way into the food that I order. For instance, I
like my salads with bacon bits. My friend asks me why I don't also
order it with turkey, saying, "You can eat that, Mike."

The waitress looks on confused, and asks why I wouldn't be able
to eat something. I tell her that he's referring to prescribed dietary
restrictions of my religion that forbid the consuming of pork - which
makes the matter of my ordering bacon bits even more difficult to
understand.

Now I'm aware that being Jewish isn't all that difficult in our
society. Once a white patient here in Tennessee told me that he

couldn't live in Los Angeles because so many people of different ethnicities reside there that he felt like a minority.

I said that I liked that about L.A., and felt less like a minority there. At that point my patient looked at me confused, and asked why I'd feel like a minority, since I was obviously white. I said that it was because I was Jewish.

"Oh," he said. "Well, you're just another kind of white."

In Tennessee I have not encountered any open racial hostility. On the contrary, this community has only greeted me with kindness and acceptance where my faith is concerned.

Let me ask you some questions, though: What if this Jewish person (me) were to attempt to move beyond religion, and seek to capture the essence of Christmas songs? Could you still accept my separate identity? Or is it too bizarre and unnatural?

When I sing, "Do You Hear What I Hear," I think about impoverished children who need help, and the possibility of people and leaders realizing these children's plight, and reaching out to them.

Now, I'm painfully aware of the song's allusion to the baby Jesus. But, tell me - Could you accept my meaning?

Or am I just a Jewish apologist, looking for a way to find acceptance, and willing to forsake his identity to fit in?

Postscript:

After this piece came out in the paper, I received a number of favorable responses, with people either expressing their solidarity with my sentiments, or wanting to learn more about Judiasm.

Still, my favorite comment came from Cathy's youngest daughter, Calista, who answered the question I posed this way:

"Jesus was Jewish," she said. "I think it's okay for you to sing Christmas songs..."

CHAPTER THIRTY

On the question of an Arab's favorite Jew?
Michael Yanuck
Waxing Philosophical
The Paris Post-Intelligencer, Paris, Tenn., Page 2, December 5, 2008.

I guess that you could say that John Baker's efforts at "Jew-baiting" worked, because I couldn't help but bite at a line he included about Jews and Arabs. (Note: My editor actually titled this piece, 'Imam: Don't respond to Baker.' As you'll see, I had to respond.)

I'm going to interrupt my Boosalis brothers series with a modest, even if belated, Thanksgiving wish.

Reading John T. Baker's letter to the editor, "Rat race is over: The rats won," I couldn't help but notice his line about asking an Arab, "Who is your favorite Jew?"

"It is a lose, lose case," Baker wrote.

Although I initially found the comment - well - interesting, I resolved to be light-hearted, and - as a Jewish person - thought about my favorite individuals within the Islamic faith.

In a previous column ("Judge people based on their character," Sept. 21, 2006), I described my kind teacher, Dr. Abbasi Akhtar, who guided me through my internship and residency. A devout Moslem, Dr. Akhtar helped me in some of my most difficult hours of caring for patients.

"Remember, Mike," he told me. "The artist loves his work. God created every man and woman. God loves His work. And when you care for His creations, God smiles ...."

In the world of politics, among my favorite Arab leaders was the late King Hussein of Jordan, who, after a Jordanian policeman shot and killed three Israeli children on the border, the King went to the homes of the grieving families, entering on his knees.

For Thanksgiving, I attended a joint service of Christians, Moslems and Jews.

After the service, we gathered for a brunch, and I went to the Imam, the Moslem prayer leader, and described Baker's letter, and then asked if he had a favorite Jew.

I was hoping that he'd respond by saying something humorous like, "My favorite is Barbra Streisand, because she sings so well."

Instead, the Imam smiled, but looked sad, and recommended that I refrain from responding to Baker's piece. Both the Rabbi and Reverend - who were still present - expressed agreement, and supported their colleague's opinion.

But some of the service participants, who witnessed the exchange, confronted me with concern and frustration.

"Mike, your question was out of context," one said. "The Imam is not Arab. He comes from Senegal. You wound up reinforcing the stereotype that all Moslems are Arabs."

Others came to my defense.

"I think that Mike was just trying to put a human face on the issue," a woman said. "A lot of people have never met an Arab or a Moslem, and all they know about them is what they see on TV."

Another woman summed up the Imam's reticence to respond directly to Baker's quote this way: "Maybe that was the Imam's way of saying, 'If something stinks, don't stir it up.'"

But it's difficult for me to keep from expressing my feelings. We all inhabit the same world, and striving for compassion and understanding and living in peace offers so much more than making jokes that suggest there's no hope for cooperation between people of certain faiths and races.

"In this country, Moslems have become the new scapegoats," a participant of the service said. "If you wear a headdress, the first thing that a lot of Americans think is that you're a terrorist."

"Colin Powell said it best," this participant continued. "When Powell was asked on 'Meet the Press' about the issue of Barrack Obama's religion, he responded, 'The question isn't whether Senator Obama is a Moslem or a Christian. The real question is: In this country, what does it matter?'"

All of us know that in our not-so-distant past, many were judged based on the color of their skin rather than the content of their character. Seemingly, with the election of our new president, we have taken a huge step away from that stain.

Now, it appears that the same needs to be achieved for our citizens of the Islamic faith.

Since the birth of this nation, the world has looked to the United States to see if people of all colors, races and religions truly can live together. Will we continue to lead the way?

With nuclear warheads pointed in every conceivable direction in places like the Middle East and elsewhere, it might be that a great deal depends on our example.

Postscript:

Mr. Baker later responded to my column, saying, "the favorite Jew line was not written with any malice toward any race, creed or color. The doctor who replaced my heart valve was a Jew; without him, I would be dead. I lived in South Florida among many Jews, who told Jewish jokes all the time."

"Accusing me of harming the world's safety by my Arab-Jew remark," he continued, "reminds me of a joke about a hillbilly boy in school. The teacher asked him, 'Who killed Abe Lincoln?' The boy said, 'I didn't do it.' The teacher asked the boy's father to come to school about his son's remark. The father said, 'My son doesn't lie. If he said he didn't kill this Lincoln feller, he didn't do it.' So, Dr. Yanuck, I am sure you are a kind and loving person. But it's not my fault that Arabs and Jews cannot live in peace. I didn't do it."

I called Mr. Baker and apologized for using his "Jew line" to make a statement, but still offered my hope that one day Jews and Arabs will live together in peace.

CHAPTER THIRTY-ONE

I resolve to have faith in the future.
Michael Yanuck
Waxing Philosophical
The Paris Post-Intelligencer, Paris, Tenn., Page 2, January 13, 2009.

After reading Mr. John Baker's latest letter to the editor ["Arab/Jew hatred not my fault," Dec. 30], I called him on the phone.

He was kind, and said that he enjoyed my column, and it made me partially regret having chosen to comment on his "joke."

But, despite his view of the "cold, hard facts of Arabs and Jews hating one another," I still believe we must continue to strive for a world in which all live in peace and brotherhood.

During the holidays, I celebrated Hannukah with some Israeli friends.

"I was born in Israel," a young woman told me. "But when I was five years old, my parents decided to move back to the United States, where they were from.

"Growing up here, I was constantly searching for where I belonged in the world. Then, when I was 17, I went back to Israel. Those were my people. Of course, I was going to connect with them, right? Wrong!

"In Israel, it was all about extremes, and fighting between different groups. The ultra-religious hate the other populations of Jews there. But because of the parliamentary system, their views influence everything.

"There was nothing that I could do about it. You tell me, what could I do? What can anybody do?"

Sometimes, living true to your beliefs does not always guarantee acceptance; nevertheless, you endeavor to heal - not just individuals, but, also, the societal ills that confront you.

With Israeli jets dropping bombs over Gaza, there's never been a more important time.

And, sure, idealism is not without its perils. My patriotic overtures to serve the country's poor have left me temporarily unable to care for veterans suffering from post-traumatic stress disorder.

As of late, while looking for a site to fulfill my federal obligation, my friend's grandmother became gravely ill. The grandmother had survived the Holocaust, and I wanted my friend to be near her in her final days.

The grandmother lives in Connecticut, and I was accepted for work in New Haven, caring for the indigent while training budding physicians at Yale. The clinic appealed to a representative of Congress, so that I would be allowed to work there. I was pledging myself to what would have been the hardest work of my life, and, yet, the National Health Service Corps still rejected it because the location was not remote enough.

"The federal government bureaucracy does not, if I may say so, give a d--- about your domestic circumstances, including the fact that your fiancee's grandmother survived the Holocaust," I was told. "It cares about the daily medical holocaust in this country and its ability to exact work from you in venues it deems particularly needy ...."

The experience of the past year has been costly, but it's given me a feeling for the difficulties of being out of work and looking for a job, and the legalistic snafus that can entangle people, and the problems that arise from them.

And who knows, maybe, there is a place out there - as yet unknown - where I can be of greater assistance. Hopefully, those in charge know what they're doing, and I'll be attending to patients soon.

Perhaps, my New Year's resolution will be to have more faith in the future, and tend less towards bitterness, fear, disappointment and regret.

For those of you who have been reading this column, thank you. You've provided me with an invaluable source of support, and I'm grateful.

Postscript:

The responses to this piece left me stunned; I had no idea of the deep emotion being stirred by the conflict in Gaza.

"Gaza is in the Biblical sense, a revelation of loss of covenant, a profound sin," one reader wrote. "And the consequences you point out compassionately (you have a knack for hitting hard, and healing at the same time!) include other victims, including the soldiers who follow orders, and come back, ruined by the PTSD. This is a tragedy for everyone but the weapons manufacturers and those whose careers profit from war.

"Your article gets to the heart of these issues, and is courageous. You risk marginalization by speaking out. You do it anyway..."

CHAPTER THIRTY-TWO

One man reached for the stars and survived his cancer.
Michael Yanuck
Waxing Philosophical
The Paris Post-Intelligencer, Paris, Tenn, Page 2, May 1st, 2009.

Last week, my friend and I were invited to a night of karaoke featuring music from Israel.

Not long after arriving, I was greeted by a man who in build, complexion and outward manner was not unlike my father.

"You sing good," Natan said. "Really, you do. You know Hebrew? How did you learn?"

I told him that I had lived in Israel for a year while working at the Weizmann Institute of Science.

"What did you study at the Weizmann Institute?" he asked.

I had studied mutations in cancer, which, later, lead to research in cancer vaccines.

"Oh, I have an interest in this kind of thing!" he said, excited. "You know why?! It's because I had cancer, cancer of the prostate. The aggressive kind. When I was diagnosed, it had already spread all over my body.

"Yes, my doctor only gave me one year to live. The only reason that I'm here is because I enrolled in an experimental protocol."

In that study, Natan had been administered massive doses of testosterone.

Typically, testosterone causes prostate cancer to grow, and usually treatment involves targeting that hormone, so as to slow the progress of the disease.

But, in Natan's case, testosterone was used to thoroughly

activate the cancer cells. After that, high dose chemo- and radio-therapy was administered to kill those charged cells.

"The treatments lasted for nine months, with potent chemotherapy," Natan said, "and then, non-stop radiation for three month afterwards."

"You know that it was only in Auschwitz-Berkinow that they tattooed you. Nowhere else did they tattoo you that way. In all the other camps, they just gave you a number."

My friend responded that she knew this, as the surviving member of her family, Gerta, had also been in Auschwitz, and had such a tattoo.

"I see," Natan replied to my friend. "So, I'm curious. How did the two of you meet?"

My friend and I had met while I was working on the cancer vaccine at the National Institutes of Health. After that, we hadn't spoken for almost 15 years.

Then, while writing for the paper, a woman introduced herself, and said that she had a story that she wanted to share with my readers. It was about how she got back together with her long lost love after 40 years.

Listening to this woman, I thought about my friend, and decided to write her a letter.

"Ahh," Natan responded in a sentimental tone. "So you listened to this couple's story, and you thought, 'Maybe there's a star out there for me, too.'

"And you found your star. You're very lucky."

Then, he looked from side to side, and edged closer.

"You know, I have a story like yours," he whispered. "It's personal, but I tell you anyway..."

(To be continued.)

CHAPTER THIRTY-THREE

Natan's second chance.
Michael Yanuck
Waxing Philosophical
The Paris Post-Intelligencer, Paris, Tenn, Page 2, May 8th, 2009.

Last week, I described a man who resembled my father, and had survived an aggressive form of cancer by enduring a grueling experimental protocol.

At the point that I left off, he had begun to confide a personal account of his life. This is his story, in his own words:

When I was young and still lived in Israel, I fell in love. Her name was Rachel. She was 16 and I was 20. Two years later, when I finished my military service, she said, "Why don't we get married?"

But I had other ideas. I had plans to study business in the United States, and, maybe, make it big there. So, I left, and, while in America, I married someone else. She got married, too. Both of us had kids.

But, through the years, we stayed in touch. Once a year, I'd go back to Israel, and usually we'd get together. Just friends, but close, like we could tell each other anything.

Then, I got divorced. After that, I was diagnosed with cancer. When my doctors said that I only had a year to live, I made a trip to Israel.

There were all kinds of things that I had to do, but when the plane landed, I just had the feeling like I wanted to talk to Rachel before I did anything else.

So I called her. When she answered the phone, I said, "Rachel, if it's OK, I need to talk with you."

"Really?!" she said. "Because I can use your help."

By this time, she was very successful, and had a real estate business. She had also divorced, and was going out with all kinds of guys.

In particular, there was this big-shot doctor - very famous in Israel - who kept calling her. That night, she and this doctor had been separately invited to the same party, because they had the same circle of friends.

"Why don't you come," she tells me, "so I can say that you're my date."

So, I came, and we laughed, we sang, we danced; the famous doctor keeps away from her, and we have a good time.

"Thank you, Natan, you really saved me," she says at the end of the party. "But when you called, you said something about needing to talk. What is it?"

So, I told her about the cancer, and that I'd been given a year to live. And that I'd come to Israel to tell my parents that this would probably be the last time we'd see each other, and I wasn't sure how to say that.

"No, Natan," she says. "You're not going to die in a year. I have plans for you for the next forty."

So, she sold off her part of the business, and came back with me to America, and we found the experimental protocol.

After a year, when it looked like I was going to live, my son says, "Dad, when are you going to marry Rachel?"

I wanted to marry her, but, with so much going on, I wasn't sure when to ask.

"Well, since the two of you got back together on January first," my son says, "why don't you get married then?"

So, we did, and here I am.

o o o o o

Natan shrugs, concluding his tale as though it were nothing out of the ordinary.

I, on the other hand, stood speechless, pondering the depths of his courage and shining example of grace, fortitude and strength.

For truly, the man standing before me had reached for his "star," and acquired not just a second chance at life, but also, at love.

Postscript: I had considered concluding this piece by challenging the readers to act with heroism equal to Natan's;

100

however, considering the conservative attitudes in Paris and the fact that Natan had divorced, I left that unsaid.

My years in Connecticut, where I knew Natan, were difficult, and, at times, I felt that I had to stop writing, and focus solely on my medical career. Oddly, in those times, Natan would find his way back into my life, like the night of a Jewish Film Festival when I shared one of my stories in response to a film about a Jewish American couple who went to Oppenheim, Germany to live, and were the first Jews to re-enter that community since the Holocaust. After the event, Natan wrote me the following:

"Dearest Michael, Your English is wonderful and very profound. Your words comes out like a story. I know that being married puts some limitations, without having an extra space. Trying to find a position which will suit you as a doctor will temporary block and put some stress in your ability and desire to write - but believe me, Mr. Yanuck, everything in your life will come to its own place like a puzzle, and you'll be able to pursue your wishes and dreams. I know you so little, but something about you makes me feel close to you. I think you are a great and special person, with high levels of modesty which you're hiding behind. Such a wonderful quality will help you in a long run. I am certain that one day you will not only be successful as a physician, but also as a great story teller (thanks to the love and passion to write which you were born with).
I want to be there to say "I told you so"!!! Much love - Natan."

In writing thus, Natan provided me with just the medicine I needed to keep my dreams alive.

CHAPTER THIRTY-FOUR

Gender equality remains elusive.
Michael Yanuck
Waxing Philosophical
The Paris Post-Intelligencer, Paris, Tenn., Page 2, March 26th, 2010.

The film, "Bruriah," begins in macabre fashion, with a group of men participating in the book-burning of a Hebrew text.

But this isn't the usual group of suspects that you'd imagine involved in such a book-burning. Rather than followers of Hitler, these are ultra-Orthodox rabbis.

What are "people of the book" doing burning a book? Hidden in the darkness, a scared little girl seems to be entertaining the same question.

Finally, she can watch no longer, and goes dashing for the flames. She tries to recover a copy of the book, only to incur serious burn wounds. The injury will scar her for life.

This is "Bruriah," a story that is to Judaism what Shakespeare's "King Lear" is to English literature.

The roots of the story come from the second century, when the rabbis declared that "women are light-minded." In that time, Bruriah was a sage who was both the wife and daughter of rabbis, renowned for her knowledge and wit.

However, even in the face of her obviously respected position, her husband, Rabbi Meir, adhered to this disparaging Talmudic assertion about women.

Then, to prove his wife's weaker nature, Rabbi Meir sent one of his students to seduce Bruriah.

Bruriah was seduced, and when she discovered that it had been planned by her husband, she committed suicide.

Horrified, Rabbi Meir ended his days in self-imposed exile in Babylonia.

Now, in the film, this story is revisited: The name of the burned little girl is Bruriah; and the burning book that she had tried to recover is titled The Seduction of Bruriah, and had been written by her brilliant rabbi father, who would be excommunicated from the ultra-Orthodox community because of its publication.

Finally, there are two more characters of significance, the high rabbi who directs the book-burning; and the high rabbi's son, Yakov, who conceals himself from sight throughout the ordeal, but nonetheless sees everything.

Both father and son are struck by Bruriah's courage - so much so that the high rabbi secretly removes a single copy of the forbidden book from the embers and, years later, the son would break with his father by marrying Bruriah.

Now, as adults, Bruriah and Yakov struggle to raise a family; however, both are still scarred from the book-burning of their childhood.

"Why was the story hidden?" Bruriah asks her husband. "If they really managed to prove that 'women are light-headed' the story should have been publicized ...."

Bruriah wants to find the book and study it. Yakov, meanwhile, wants no part of it.

"The tree of life and the tree of knowledge are the same tree," Yakov retorts.

Yakov is still clinging to his ultra-Orthodox heritage, and trying to instill those values in his children.

This is especially true for his eldest daughter, who has just announced that she wants to become a rabbi - something that is strictly forbidden in ultra-Orthodox tradition.

Adding fuel to this combustible mixture is the introduction of a handsome, young rabbinical student. Sasha, who is intensely interested in the story of Bruriah, and set on discovering the mystery of the night of the book-burning, and the identity of the burned text.

"It has everything," Sasha says of Bruriah. "Betrayal, death, God ... sex."

Indeed, in Judaism, sexual intimacy within the bounds of marriage is considered a spiritual experience. This is perhaps because it involves the creation of new life, and therefore, touches on the divine. In addition, sexuality is linked to a certain sense of knowledge, as observed in Genesis: "... and Adam knew his wife

Eve."

Sasha teaches at the Yakovs' school, and Yakov takes an instant disliking to him.

Then, Sasha meets Bruriah at a bookshop, and their common search for the forbidden text unites them.

Ultimately, the relationship of Yakov and Bruriah is pushed to the breaking point, and Yakov appeals to his distant father - the high rabbi who sanctioned the book-burning - for help.

In response, Yakov's father reaches behind the Arc of the Covenant, brandishes the lone existing copy of the burned text and delivers it into his son's hands.

Yakov, in turn, gives the book to the student, Sasha. When Sasha shares the book with Bruriah, she turns to him for comfort and solace.

Then, Sasha reveals to Bruriah that the book came to him through her husband, and she leaves in a fit of despair.

Yakov hunts for his wife. When he finds her, Bruriah appears reduced to a strumpet wandering the forlorn streets of Jerusalem.

Yakov follows Bruriah to the outskirts of the Holy City. Then, at an outdoor pool atop a hill, she disappears.

Yakov removes his clothing and enters the water, as though to purify himself. Then, Bruriah reveals herself and joins him in the pool.

Now, cleansed of the past, perhaps they can finally really know each other - and choose life over oblivion.

CHAPTER THIRTY-FIVE

The Shattering of Glass.
Michael Yanuck
Waxing Philosophical
The Paris Post-Intelligencer, Paris, Tenn.

In this piece, I offer a stream-of-consciousness rendering of the thoughts and feeling that I experienced on my wedding day.

Time waits for none, particularly where my friend is concerned.

We arrange a relatively large gathering; me secretly hoping that the presence of those most significant in my life might help me to find my way.

But even on the eve of the event, I'm still unresolved.

Then, my friend admits that she, too, has concerns about commitment.

"Maybe, we could just tell everyone that we decided to stay friends," she says, "and to try to enjoy the party anyway."

In the Jewish tradition, the event concludes with the shattering of a glass. The origins of this ritual are not precisely known. Many scholars believe that it commemorates the destruction of the Temple, so that even on the most joyous of occasions, that happening is still remembered.

But, really, I don't want any part of it. My life to be about creating, I tell myself, not destroying.

I'd seen enough of that. In my early years, I'd been a not impassive observer to the death of my relative's long time girlfriend, Nickie, whom he loved.

Could he have saved her?

Going to my friend's father, I confide my concerns, saying that the home in which I'd been raised in was quite different from the home that he had made for his children.

He nods, and offers simply, "It was what you were taught."

But how do you un-teach that? How do you un-learn, so to guard Heaven's last best gift?

The rabbi hands me the glass, and laying it on the ground and kneeling before it, a myriad of thoughts whirl in my head.

Is it possible that I might be forgiven, and that the glass' sacrifice might serve to remind me that relationships are fragile, and can be shattered if trampled under foot.

And as I rise, I realize that that kind of destruction is within me, and it's for me to choose between creation and oblivion.

And with a force of conviction that I did not know I had, a crashing sound rang out, and all cried, "Mazel tov."

CHAPTER THIRTY-SIX

Reservation like Nazi camps?
Michael Yanuck
Waxing Philosophical
The Paris Post-Intelligencer, Paris, Tenn., Page 2, February 4th, 2011.

Stan drove me to the home of a prominent elder named Orville White Buffalo.

"Orville was a university professor for many years," the restaurant owner said. "He just retired."

Pulling into the driveway of what looked like a rundown shack, we were greeted by an elderly but robust-looking Native American man who was just getting out of an old and rusting pickup truck.

"Hello, Orville," the restaurant owner said, and the two exchanged greetings in Lakota. "I have a doctor here," the owner said. "He would like to learn more about the reservation. I was hoping that you could talk with him."

"OK," Orville said. "I'm just getting back from the JDC. Come in."

We followed him into the house. "What's the JDC?" I asked.

"It's the juvenile detention center," the restaurant owner said. "Orville volunteers a lot of his time there."

"I'm concerned," Orville said, "because the young people there are not learning the language and stories of our people." Orville sat heavily at the kitchen table.

"When I spend time with the gang members who are locked up there," Orville continued, "I tell them, 'I know that you are smart. Now, you need to work on your lives to direct that intelligence in a positive way.'

"I say, 'There is good and bad in all of us. It's a choice, whether we are going to band together to make a lot of trouble in the world, or if we're going to go out and do a lot of good. Use this time to plan for the good that you can do once you're out of these walls.'"

My thoughts drifted to the Holocaust survivor and writer, Dr. Viktor Frankl.

"Viktor Frankl had been a successful psychiatrist and brain surgeon," I said. "But in the concentration camp, he felt like little more than an animal. All he thought about all day was food — to the point that he felt he might kill for a scrap of bread.

"Then one day, he had an insight. He thought, 'I'm a psychiatrist, and in this miserable place, I have an opportunity to closely observe those in the worst of circumstances. Here I can learn about human behavior under conditions that would appear to be overwhelming, and perhaps, should I survive, I can share that knowledge.'

"And, from that time on, his life in Auschwitz was transformed. He let go of hunger, and looked forward to each new day, despite the horrors."

Orville had listened in silence, his eyes directed downward. I thought that I had carried on too long, and thereby, worn out my welcome.

"I think that the reservation was a kind of concentration camp," Orville said, finally. "Those in charge made sure that all we had was a third-grade education, and taught complete dependence on authority."

To be continued.

Postscript:

I deliberately included the description of Orville's home as a "shack" because of the popular book of the same name that a number of my Paris friends were reading. In fact, one of my evangelical readers had sent me a copy.

The Shack has been described as "a one of a kind invitation to journey to the very heart of God," and I was hoping this feeling would carry over to Orville's home and heart.

Really, though, I don't think that my editor was particularly helpful on this score when he chose to introduce the column with the doubtful title.

As for the Reservation being like a concentration camp, my wife was of the opinion that it was more comparable to a ghetto. "You have this people that by race is being called in and pulled from the rest of the land and put into this one place - that's the ghetto part of it," she said. "But there weren't gas chambers or ovens where the bodies were being burned."

"The whole scale, cold-blooded slaughter of the Native American race was something that this country couldn't quite do," she continued. "It was something that they were basically doing, but they couldn't quite pull the trigger on the last ones - unlike the Nazis, where the extermination of the Jews was a part of their stated purpose. I think there were people in this country who wanted to do it, but couldn't quite stomach it and were being pulled back from the brink. There was a stated purpose of gaining their lands, though. People wanted their land."

"So I think a lot of the deaths happened before [the Reservations]," she concluded. "You have Wounded Knee still happening at the time that the Lakota have been put on the Reservations, but after the people settled in the Reservations, there was misery, but a lot of the actual physical killing stopped - though the spiritual killing started."

CHAPTER THIRTY-SEVEN

On transformations and Lakota way, based on outcome
Michael Yanuck
Waxing Philosophical
The Paris Post-Intelligencer, Paris, Tenn., Page 2, March 18th, 2011.

After the Sweat Lodge ceremony, I was invited to share in a meal with the others, and sat and talked with Orville White Buffalo.

"Every Lakota family on the reservation has been touched be suicide," he said. "I want to help those that had attempted suicide to choose life over death, and remind them how awesome it was to be a human being."

I told him that I had found the sweat lodge ceremony healing, and that it seemed to help me reconcile fears from a childhood experience in which I'd nearly drowned.

Orville nodded. "The lodge is about resolving trauma by being reborn," he said. "It's about going back into the womb of the mother, and being nourished that way, and then re-emerging from the womb — so that there's more bonding and more love as a result of your participation in the ceremony."

"It took me a long time to understand these things," he continued. "My father was a Medicine man, but he died when I was nine, before I could understand a lot of his teachings.

"After he died, I was sent away to boarding school, where we were forbidden from speaking the Lakota language.

"When the missionaries caught us speaking our native tongue, they'd pulled at our ears so hard that they nearly come away from our skulls. I'm not just saying that. There are some of us who can show you the scars.

"Later in college, I took classes in Greek and Hebrew, so that I could study the ancient Judeo-Christian texts. I was trying to understand why the missionaries thought their way was the only way, and to do things anyone else's way meant eternal damnation, and why our ways were never so much as considered.

"In 1972, I was studying in Germany. That was the year that terrorists from Black September invaded the Olympic compound and killed members of the Israeli team.

"After the massacre, I visited the Dachau concentration camp, and studied about the Holocaust. Then, when I returned to the reservation, I performed a ritual Sundance. It's a ceremony where you fast over four-day intervals for as many as 16 days.

"At the end of the fast, I had a vision. I saw three women being gassed, and even in the gas chamber, they were singing. And their song was so beautiful that it haunted their executioners, until their executioners gave up their dogmatic practices, and stopped gassing people."

I told him that most of my friend's family had perished in the Holocaust.

"The one survivor left was a cousin named Hanne," I said, "who had been a hidden child during World War II. She doesn't talk much about it. She calls herself an 'anti-hero' because she survived."

"I once heard Elie Weisel (Holocaust survivor and Nobel Prize winner)," Orville said. "He told people, 'I am not a hero. I survived. I would have eaten my grandmother's bread if I could.'

"'The heroes,' Weisel said, 'were the ones who gave of their own bread. They were the heroes.' And you know what happened to them — most of them did not survive."

Indeed, I had heard about such heroes.

Ruth Klemens, the woman who knew Anne Frank in Amsterdam and then at the Bergen-Belson concentration camp, had told me her mother had given her bread to her and her sister, then fought for her daughter's freedom ("Ruth Klemen's mother was a hero, saving her daughters," The Post-Intelligencer, April 16, 2010). She died shortly after their release.

"What does your wife do for a living?" Orville asked.

"She's an art conservator," I said. "She worked at the Museum of the American Indian."

"I went to the museum," Orville responded. "I took my daughter there. We went to collect the remains of an Indian girl who had been murdered."

"This was supposed to be pre-contact with the whites," he continued. "But when we looked at the bones, we saw saber marks.

"The marks were right there on the skull of the young girl. When my daughter saw them, she cried and cried."

His daughter's experience reminded me of my own at the Holocaust museum.

"When I learned that there was more than just cruelty in the years of World War II," I said, "and that there had been some Germans who had risked their lives to save Jews, I searched for a dark place in the shadows, and then wept and wept.

"It was as though a switch had been thrown in my head," I continued. "I'd conditioned myself to believe that hatred and murder was just the norm during the Holocaust and to be expected.

"But that day in the museum taught me that the potential for kindness is always there, and acting with compassion is a choice; and being good to each other is worth fighting for, and cruelty and intolerance is never to be accepted."

"You are talking about transformation," Orville responded, moved. "In the Lakota way, we do not judge based on right and wrong. Instead, we ask, 'What is the outcome?'"

"Because you never know what the outcome of something will be," he concluded, "and have to allow for experiences that are transforming."

To be continued.

Postscript:

My conversation with "Orville" actually ran deeper than that described here, but the contents were very personal and I believed that they limited me to the submission rendered.

"I feel blessed for having had this conversation with you," Orville told me. "I can tell in your voice that your way is humble and there is humility in your tone, but it does not keep you from being willing to act, as you do when you speak your mind and state what you believe in, as you have done with me."

When I shared the contents of this conversation with my wife, she described an interesting coincidence; it involved her long-time friend, Robert, a Native American who had worked with her at the Museum of the American Indian.

"If this man you were talking with went to the Museum to repatriate that young girl's skeleton," she said, "then he would have

met Robert.   Because Robert was responsible for packaging all of the re-patriated skeletons before shipment..."

CHAPTER THIRTY-EIGHT

Elderly doctor nears retirement
Michael Yanuck
Waxing Philosophical
The Paris Post-Intelligencer, Paris, Tenn, Page 2, April 17th, 2011.

Frank's niece had been attended to by an older physician named Dr. Curtiz. After seeing to her care, Curtiz approached me.

"I understand that you're a doctor," he said, "and that you're interested in working here."

I said that I was curious about the place, and asked what had brought him here.

"Well, I came here after Vietnam," he said. "Like a lot of veterans coming home from the war, I just wanted to go someplace where I could be away from people, and that's how I wound up in here.

"Still, I'm rather proud of what I've been able to do here. Last year, I was ranked 17th in the state in caring for the indigent and underserved.

"Recently, my daughter got married. My new son-in-law's father was also a doctor. He graduated from Loma Linda, and when I met him, he talked about how proud he was that he'd never taken care of an indigent patient, and all his patients had private insurance.

"I listened and thought, 'And you're a graduate of Loma Linda. A fine Jesuit university. What kind of Christian values are those?' Loma Linda is where I went to medical school, too.

"Anyway, when I originally came here, there were sixteen doctors serving the reservation. Now, we're down to three.

"But that's how it was in the war years. Back then, when they had the draft and you came here; you had a party because you weren't in Vietnam. Now that they took away the draft and you don't have to be here except if you're paying back student loans, then there's no reason to be here, and everybody's left. In general, there's no feeling for public service anymore, and no one to take care of this population. It kind of worries me, being that I'm planning on retiring in a few years.

"My wife and I will probably stay here, although we like to travel. For our last anniversary, we took a trip to Europe and visited a number of Holocaust sites. We visited Anne Frank's annex. Then, we went to Auschwitz and saw all the tremendous crematoriums there — all created for just one purpose, to murder other human beings.

"The highlight of the trip was going to the workshop of Oskar Schindler. There, I had the honor of sitting at Schindler's desk. It was the same desk that he never left — not one night — for all the time that he was in charge of the Jews who worked in his factory, until he finally he had to leave — and run for it.

"He failed most every business venture he ever entered, especially after the war — he was never a success by any standards.

"But he saved 1,500 human lives — all of those who worked for him. It just goes to show how this very human figure could wind up doing the most extraordinary of things."

To be continued.

Postscript:

Dr. Curtiz is a composite character inspired by many dedicated physicians on the Rosebud Reservation; however, this submission was particularly influenced by dentist, Dr. James Szana. While performing a rather difficult series of dental procedures on me, Dr. Szana shared his journey to comprehend the Holocaust. He was a non-Jew, born in this country, and whose life had not been directly affected by the Holocaust. Yet, he took it upon himself to travel to Europe, and journey from the annex of Anne Frank in Amsterdam, to the crematoriums of Auschwitz in Poland, and, ultimately, the office of German businessman, Oskar Schindler, who inspired him most of all because "he was a man who never really amounted to much in his profession, yet he saved thousands of lives, and slept at that desk every night until the end of the war."

As a Jew, the Holocaust is a significant part of my consciousness, awareness and what it means to be here; however, I don't know that I would have looked as deeply at the Holocaust had I not been Jewish.

Dr. Szana's interest showed me that the Holocaust might have meaning to more than just the members of my race, and perhaps that event inspired others to a call for humanitarian service. Indeed, this collection was inspired in a large part by Dr. Szana, whose storytelling captivated me from first we met; it even made a difficult dental procedure something to look forward to. In describing his search for understanding - and by speaking with such humanity and compassion - Dr. Szana did much to allay my fears, and made an otherwise painful procedure pass quickly; it spoke volumes about his quality as a human being, and in that way inspired the rendering of this collection.

CHAPTER THIRTY-NINE

Doctor: We didn't meet by coincidence
Michael Yanuck
Waxing Philosophical
The Paris Post-Intelligencer, Paris, Tenn, Page 2, April 22nd, 2011.

"My own ethnic background is Hungarian," Dr. Curtiz said. "In the waning months of the World War II, the number of Hungarian Jews who were shipped to Auschwitz and murdered was 500,000. To get an idea of the enormity of that, think of this — in all of WWII, the United States lost 300,000 soldiers — well under the number of Jews murdered from Hungary alone."

I was moved by his reflections, and offered him some Holocaust material that I had written. The next day, Curtiz gave me a call.

"Thank you for sharing your stories with me," he said. "I enjoyed very much your style and compassion as you relayed your encounters. In a short time, you were able to get to the heart of the matter with warmth and understanding.

"I would like to spend some time together," he continued. "We have a lot to talk about. I have many questions to ask you, and some things I would like to share. It is not my nature to believe in coincidence. It is my opinion that however you happened into my 'mission field' of 35 years, it was supposed to occur.

"I know nothing of your schedule, but we need to figure out a way to get to know each other. Are you available for lunch?"

To be continued.

Postscript:

Dr. James Szana was perhaps the greatest natural storyteller I ever met. From the beginning, I hung on his every word. No one had ever articulated and helped me understand the horrific scale of the mass murder committed during the Holocaust than he did. It was a horrifying account of the systematic murder perpetrated.

CHAPTER FORTY

Doctor discusses Holocaust trip
Michael Yanuck
Waxing Philosophical
The Paris Post-Intelligencer, Paris, Tenn, Page 2, April 29th, 2011.

    Dr. Curtiz and I met at Stan's restaurant. After being seated at a table, he passed me a photograph.

    "It's one of my proudest possessions," Curtiz said. "A photo of me writing in the guest book at Schindler's office just outside of Krakow. Most nights he slept in that office, so that he could be sure that nothing would happen to the Jews who he had working for him. If you look straight ahead, you could view his factory buildings. It was an awesome honor to be there."

    I looked at the picture, then asked how he'd become interested in the Holocaust.

    "Since I can remember," he began, "I've always had this interest in what in the world could have happened in the minds of people to carry out such a terrible death program for other human beings? I didn't get it. In a period of three months, 400,000 Jews in Hungary were murdered. They were put on trains, and they went straight up from there to Auschwitz or Berkenau.

    "My grandpa didn't live very far from one of those train stations. He left Hungary in 1905. He was the only one in his family who left. His mother and father wanted him to leave, and come to the land of opportunity.

    "And he did. He came to New York. I don't know what he did in

New York, but after a while, he came to Toledo … (and) he met another Hungarian woman, and they got married.

"But, for no reason, after Grandma and Grandpa got married, they became Seventh-day Adventists. And that was interesting because both came over from a predominantly Catholic country ….

"And Seventh-day Adventists are protestant Christians who worship on Saturday, and Sabbath begins on Friday night at sundown and lasts until Saturday night at sundown. The night before Saturday, our shoes were shined and ready for church. We had everything done before sundown.

"Seventh-day Adventists follow Levitus 11, and they don't eat shellfish, vultures or swine. It's the same as Kosher laws. They don't celebrate Jewish holidays, but Saturday Sabbath is central to the Seventh-day Adventist. And because of the dietary principles, a lot of Adventists are vegetarian.

"So my grandparents became members of the Seventh-day Adventists — probably the closest protestant Christian church to Jewish in terms of how they conducted their lives.

"Then Grandpa, of all things, became a caretaker in a Jewish cemetery. That was his job. So of course, Grandpa knew all the people in the Jewish community. This is in Toledo, and the cemetery wasn't huge, but it was big enough to hire someone to be the caretaker."

"Now, my grandfather got correspondence from Hungary," Curtiz continued. "He got letters from his parents, his cousins. But after World War II, Grandpa didn't get letters from anybody in the 'Old Country,' as he called it.

"In 1985, I had the opportunity to go to Hungary, and I begged my dad to come with me. I said, 'You understand Hungarian. You grew up speaking that language. I'd like you to come because at least you'd know something.'

"And he said, 'Absolutely not. No, I won't go there.' And he is not that kind of a person. It was the most unusual thing for him to say.

"Then, I had the opportunity to do some teaching for a while. I taught for the United States Medical Institute, going between 25 cities all around the country … just all over the place.

"Well, one of my co-instructors was Norman Silver, who was a fabulous instructor and who was Jewish. One time I was telling him about my grandfather, and how he worked at the Jewish cemetery.

"Well, after I got through talking, Norman says, 'Jim, I'm taking you out to dinner tonight.'

"I said, 'Good, where are we going?'

"He says we are going to a restaurant approved by the rabbis. 'We're going to have Jewish food,' he says.

"I said, 'I didn't know there was Jewish food.'

"He says, 'Well, yeah, there is — kind of.'

"So we go in there and sit down, and they had two different sampler plates, and it was quite a selection of food, and he says, 'I'm going to order for both of us.'

"So, he ordered both sampler plates. And then I remember him telling the waitress, 'We are so hungry, we are just going to eat like pigs.'

"So, they start bringing this food. And the first dish came by, and I recognized it, and I said, 'Wow, this is Hungarian food, because this is what Grandma made.

And he said, 'It's not Hungarian food.'

"And almost every single thing that was brought out on the sampler was stuff that my Grandma made. And it was Hungarian food to me — and that included some of the desserts and rolls with nuts that Grandma called 'birdies' — the whole thing.

"And he said, 'Jim, that is not Hungarian food. That's Jewish food.'

Postscript:

In "Dr. Curtiz" I felt that I'd found the best aspects of Judaism and Christianity.

I viewed Jesus was as a rabbi who had meant to help Judaism spiritually progress from a God of fire and brimstone to One of love.

CHAPTER FORTY-ONE

Living under dark cloud not easy
Michael Yanuck
Waxing Philosophical
The Paris Post-Intelligencer, Paris, Tenn, Page 2, May 6th, 2011.

Listening to Dr. Curtiz, my eyes glazed over.

"Something the matter, Mike?" he asked.

"There had been a time," I said, "when my Jewish identity had been unknown to me, too."

Some of you might remember this story (I described it in a previous column, "Hitler, my country, and Will Strickland," March 24, 2008): When I was perhaps 6-7 years old, a new family moved into my neighborhood, and although the children were handsome and athletic, they seemed withdrawn and sad somehow, as though some dark cloud perpetually hung over them.

Then, one day, I overheard the older boy of this new family say, "I hate Hitler," and I went home and asked my mother who Hitler was?

She explained that our new neighbors were Jewish, and Hitler had been the leader of a group called Nazis who had rounded up the Jews and sent them to concentration camps; there, they were put into "showers" and gassed; afterwards, their remains were burned in furnaces, in flames that consumed them, until nothing was left of them, except great billows of smoke and ash rising from huge, towering chimneys into an ever-darkening sky.

122

"Listening to my mother," I told Curtiz, "my heart went out to this neighborhood boy. I felt as though I could understand him, and why he and his family were more reserved than the rest of us.

"And, in that moment, I felt a deep sense of purpose; I would dedicate myself to fight tyranny, and work to see that nothing like what happened to these Jews ever happened again. Not to anyone.

"Then, my mother told me something else. She said, 'And we're Jewish, too.'

"And in that split second, my whole world changed. That dark cloud that hung over my neighbors — well, now it was over me, too. I went from being a sunny Californian and defender of the weak, to a forlorn Jew. And all that strength and vigor that had filled me — it all drained away.

"Sometimes, I wonder, 'What if my mother hadn't told me that I was Jewish that day? What if I had never known? What if I could have grown up to be that other person, the one who sought to be an advocate for the oppressed, just because it felt like the right thing to do?'"

I looked at Dr. Curtiz. "What if my mother hadn't told me that I was Jewish," I repeated, "just as it seems that your father never told you?"

Curtiz studied me.

"Maybe, it's time to get out from under that cloud," he said.

I shook my head.

"How?" I asked.

"Yes, Mike," he said, nodding. "Hau."

To be continued.

Postscript:

"Hau" is, naturally, Lakota for "Hello." It was actually Dr. Dan Foster who offered this Lakota transition on the evening that he offered me a postion at the Rosebud Hospital.

I feel tremendous excitement and enthusiasm for my work with the IHS. By this work I get to fulfill the vision that I had for myself between the time that I was listening to that boy in the neighborhood say "I hate Hitler," and my mother offer the explanation for his hatred; what I felt before she informed me that I was also Jewish and I had that feeling of being helpless and afraid; when I aspired to help people in need. I'm back to that person now and realizing my fullest aspirations.

This sentiment was reinforced in my conversations with

internationally renowned author, Kent Nerburn, who wrote "Neither Wolf Nor Dog."

"As a physician, you can always make a difference," he said. "Anywhere you go, you'll be needed. But what I experienced on the Reservation was a feeling that, more than 'important,' the work that he was doing was 'essential.'"

CHAPTER FORTY-TWO

Added to Holocaust Committee
Michael Yanuck
Waxing Philosophical
The Paris Post-Intelligencer, Paris, Tenn., Page 2, November 25th, 2011.

During a stay at an Indian reservation, I was caught in a flash flood and had to be helped out of the White River. Unbeknownst to me, at the same time that I was struggling in the river, there was a rash of suicides within the reservation that took the lives of several young people. I would later learn that the rate of suicides on this reservation was among the highest in the world.

I sought answers, and met people on the reservation who were working to make a difference and attempting to reach the youth with a message of hope.

Among these people was Frank, a local artist who taught the Indian reservation children traditional Lakota art, had just been placed in jail for stabbing a man.

That scared me, and I was making arrangements to leave. Before leaving, I looked through my emails and read the following announcement:

"Ruth Klemens, beloved wife of Paul Klemens, passed away after a courageous struggle with cancer. She had been a resident of Connecticut since 1967, living first in Manchester, then in Storrs until moving to West Hartford this year.

"Although her profession was as a foreign language teacher, she was also a respected educator and frequent lecturer on the Holocaust.

"She was born in Berlin, Germany on Aug. 4, 1927, the child of

Alfred Wiener and Margaret Saulmann. In 1933, the family fled to Amsterdam to escape the growing Nazi threat, where they joined a community of other displaced Jews, and she grew up in the same Jewish community as the renown Anne Frank.

"Like Anne Frank, Ms. Klemens, too, had kept a journal, of sorts, and in it, recalled the last time she saw Anne and her sister, Margot, in a partitioned unit of the Bergen-Belsen concentration camp located next to where Ms. Klemens and her family were being held ...."

I remembered the day I was introduced to Ms. Klemens and the excitement I felt when I was told that Ms. Klemens had known Anne Frank. Here I was in my mid-40s and about to meet someone who had known Anne Frank, the young girl who had died 20 years before I was born and whose celebrated diary I had read when I was 10.

After meeting Ms. Klemens, I wrote a series of articles about her ("Anne Frank's diary helped Ruth Klemens come to terms with Holocaust," April 9-30, 2010).

I had shared those articles with a friend, Natan, who served on a Holocaust Committee. Now, I contacted Natan to tell him the news of Ms. Klemens' passing.

"I'm so sorry to find out that Ruth Klemens is not with us anymore," Natan said. "Eighty-four is quite a young age. Your story about her and Anne Frank should be sent to Yad VaShem in Israel, or perhaps the Holocaust Museum in Washington. I loved your uplifting story! You immortalized Ruth forever. You were lucky to know her."

Then, Natan surprised me.

"Michael, I have great news for you," he said. "It has been a great honor to read your precious Holocaust stories, and now I have the ability to appoint you to the Holocaust Committee. What do you think? Would you like to serve and be a part of the committee?"

Nothing could make me happier.

"Then, I will let you know the date when we're meeting," he said. "Probably in a couple days. I will introduce you to the Holocaust Committee. OK?"

I told him that it might be difficult as I was presently on an Indian reservation.

"You are at an Indian reservation?" he said, excited. "I think you are the probably the happiest man in the world. This is your destiny.

"I know that the Indians have had quite a Holocaust of their own, and I read a lot about it. I read about the Indians who were moved from Georgia to a different location; they had a long walk and about 70 percent of them died on the way. The Indians end up being killed everywhere, just because the white man so desired what was theirs. They killed a culture that lived in America for thousands of years before the first white man even came here. Terrible. I think that you are just the perfect person to be there. I want you to know that."

"When I think of what I know about the reservations in the Dakotas," he continued, "I get totally disgusted all over again with the U.S. government which stole and lied its way to the power grab and subsequent actions which led directly to such degradation and extreme poverty for these native people who had so much greater respect for life and for the earth than our so-called more 'civilized' forefathers. It would seem to me that the U.S. government owes these tribal people a whole lot more support than it will ever provide them."

"So, I thank you for all the writings," he concluded. "Just keep writing. This is the perfect place for you to write. Who knows, maybe one of these days I'll come to visit you."

Listening, I didn't have the heart to tell Natan my real thoughts and intentions, and getting off the phone, I went back to packing.

Then, there was a knock at the door. Opening it, Frank stood in the doorway.

"Michael, surprised to see me?" he said. "They just let me out. It was cold in there. They just had mats for beds — no mattresses. It was really uncomfortable. My back's hurting. Could you give me a lift home?"

To be continued.

Postscript:

At the time of Ms. Klemens' death, a sudden storm had struck New England and resulted in power outages that affected more than half the state of Connecticut where she lived. Indeed, the October nor'easter knocked out power to more than 3 million homes and business across the Northeast, including 830,000 in Connecticut, where outages exceeded those of all other states combined. The Connecticut Light & Power had called the snowstorm and resulting power outages "an historic event."

Ms. Klemens had required oxygen, and it might have been that the outages caused by the story affected the function of her breathing machine and contributed to her demise. For some like my mother-in-law (who had introduced me to Ms. Klemens), this possibility brought to mind the suffocation of Holocaust victims in the gas chambers.

Frank actually spent months in jail, it was outside a store that we met again. I don't think that I handled it very well. He said that he still had the healing staffs that I'd contracted him to work on and asked if I wanted them. I feared his potential for violence and essentially severed contact with him.

CHAPTER FORTY-THREE

Terrified, I'm hanging over a cliff
Michael Yanuck
Waxing Philosophical
The Paris Post-Intelligencer, Paris, Tenn., Page 2, December 2nd, 2011.

The passage that follows is much more dramatic than I would have like, but my editor insisted on splitting the piece into two parts and doing it in a way that would leave it a literal cliff-hanger.

Frank, a local artist who taught the Indian reservation children traditional Lakota art, had just been released from jail for stabbing a man, and asked me to give him a ride home.

But his arrest had scared me, and I was making arrangements to leave. The front seat of my car was occupied with bags, but I rearranged them to make space for him.

"Are you going someplace, Michael?" he asked. Yes, I was leaving. "Oh," he said.

We made the familiar drive along the White River. "Michael, can I ask you something?" he said. "What are your origins? Where do your people come from?"

I said that my great-grandfather came from Russia.

"Oh," he said. "Because I thought you might be Jewish." Yes, I was Jewish. "Yeah, well, you should just say so," he responded. "If it were me, I think it would be a source of pride."

My great-grandfather had left Russia after a pogrom, a violent mob attack aimed at Jews. What was there to be proud of?

"You know, I was born in the hospital here," he continued. "And the doctor who delivered me was a Jewish doctor. After the delivery, my parents asked what they could do to pay him. He said, 'You could leave that boy with me.' But my mom wouldn't do it and insisted on taking me home. Years later, when she told me, I said, 'Mom, why couldn't you have just let me go with him? I mean, I might have really made something of myself. Maybe, I could have become a doctor. Maybe, a lawyer. I would have been brought up by Jews.'"

I smiled, but he remained serious.

"Do you know much about Israel, Michael?" Frank asked.

I had lived in Israel for a year, I said.

"Is that so," he responded. "I've always been impressed that, after so many years, the Jews finally came back to their homeland, even after all the things that happened to them."

Ascending a hill, the view of the river was replaced by the arid Plains.

"Do you believe that prayer can help people, Michael?" he asked.

No, I said.

"Why?" he asked.

"Six million of my people were murdered in the Holocaust," I said. "I imagine that all of them were praying, and God never answered their prayers."

"Maybe, they weren't listening," he responded, "when the answer was to fight. My father fought in World War II. He taught me a song that he and other veterans would sing." Frank tapped on the dashboard like a drum and began to sing:

"Paha nazi yo hey natan heyapi
Iya sicha kin hey nata heyapi."

I asked what the song meant.

"It's sort of hard to explain," he said. "The Lakota language is so different that it's not easy to translate into English. The words say something like, 'Charge, the Nazi is up the hill. He holds his head as he runs. Charge, he's up the hill.'"

He leaned back and looked out at the road. "I always thought that I would follow in my father's footsteps and go into the Marines like he did," he said. "But I got into too many scraps in high school and lost my chance."

He stared ahead. "Hey, I never got to show you those burial grounds," he said. "Do you still want to see them? They're not far from my home."

He directed me to park in an open field. Getting out, we followed a trail into the woods and then along a precipice above the river. As we ventured onwards, the trail narrowed and, in parts, all but disappeared.

Frank leapt between a break in the trail. Considering that Frank was older and heavier than me, I figured that I could do the same. I took a couple steps back and then made a running jump. Frank turned.

"No, Michael, wait!" he said.

But I'd already leapt. Landing on the other side, I tried to grip the surface, but the ground beneath me gave way and I went sliding down the hillside. Frank tried to catch hold of my arm, but I was moving too fast and slipped through his grasp.

Small particles of unearthed material — dirt, stones, twigs and splinters — flew over my head as I continued to slide. With my fingers, I raked the ground in an effort to stop, but it was no use.

Then, just as the hillside divided into the cliff face, I got caught in the lifeless remains of a once-slender tree. As its barren branches tore through my shirt and flesh and brought my slide to a halt, I watched — terrified — as the gravel that had been traveling with me continued its descent over the cliff and then down some 30 feet until splashing into the river below.

I tried to achieve a toe-hold, but the ground at my feet just kept giving way.

To be continued.

Postscript:

Although "Frank" had shared a number of songs, the one cited here was actually imparted by my Lakota Music and Dance instructor, Kevin Wright. Not long before this submission, Kevin shared an interesting story of his own and spoke with great feeling about a vision that had come to him near the end of a four day Sundance ceremony, in which he'd been among the chief singers, gone without food or drink, and performed mostly in direct sun. The vision had come during a break in the ceremony, when he'd been momentarily overcome by exhaustion.

"As I turned away from the beer my grandmother was offering me, and made my return to the Sundance ceremony, I saw my father-in-law there by the window with his two hands extended above his head and holding out a chanupa [sacred, ceremonial pipe], and as I opened the door to make my way, I stepped out into this bright light."

Kevin had come from a family of alcoholics, and he, too, had been an alcoholic before coming under the sphere of his father-in-

law, a revered holy man.

"Then, at the end of the ceremony," Kevin continued, "my father-in-law had a big give-away. At the end, he called me up, saying that he wanted to honor me because of my contribution to the ceremony, and presented me with a chanupa. And it was the same chanupa that I'd seen in my dream."

Not long after this ceremony, numerous members of Kevin's family passed away from mostly alcohol-related illness, including his grandmother. It was difficult for Kevin to resist the temptation to go back to drinking, but with the aid of his father-in-law, he has remained sober.

As for the song Paha Nazi, it made me feel good to know that I was serving people who had once participated in fighting those who would have annihilated my race had they not been fought and defeated.

A number of people on the Reservation have expressed interest about my Jewish roots. Young people like "Ted" had asked questions about Israel, the persecution of the Jews, and related the history of the Jews to the experience of their people. The tribal president, Rodney Bordeaux, asked questions about Israel, as the tribe had been interested in recognizing the Jewish state. Later, Mr. Bordeaux confided that he had asked Rosebud's incoming Clinical Director, Dr. Ira Salom (who pronounced his name "Salem"), about the origins of his family name and been surprised by Dr. Salom's response.

"He said that it came from Poland or Russia," Mr. Bordeaux said. "I thought it might be Jewish, and, if it were true, I imagined that it would be a source of pride."

I thought about sharing this conversation with Dr. Salom; however, he seemed a rather private man, who insists that he is doing this work just to serve, and mostly avoided what I had to say about my interest in Native American culture and healing techniques. (More about Dr. Salem in a later book.)

Finally, where prayer is concerned, my wife is convinced that it made a difference in the locating of our current home in Chamberlain. This story begins when I got a promotion to serve as Clinical Director at the Lower Brule Reservation; however, for months my wife and I were separated because of massive flooding from the Missouri River that ran right along the Reservation. One day, during another futile effort on my wife's part to find a home for us to share, she prayed. In doing so, she missed her usual turn-off and wound up in front of a real estate office. She had been there before and was told that there were no homes available, but feeling *divinely inspired, she decided to try one more time. Not only was there a home, but they would also permit our cat, Socks, in the house (everywhere else that we had tried, we'd been told that the cat would have to be de-clawed, and I wasn't about to accept that, no matter how long my wife and I had to be separated!)*

The fall and slide described was mostly based on events in a hike with my wife near a historic site along the Lewis and Clark expedition and left my hand significantly injured.

I had objected to this piece being split this way for a number of reasons: 1. It was much too dramatic; 2. I was looking to complete this series by the end of the year, and this was limiting my chances; 3. It was placing me in the spotlight, and taking the focus away from my subject.

Finally, when the article came out, my wife reminded me that, in actuality, I had distanced myself from Frank after he left jail; she thought that it was the right thing to do considering the element of danger about him; nevertheless, had I followed my heart, I would have continued my interactions with him. "This was your alter ego doing [in the article] what you didn't do," my wife concluded.

CHAPTER FORTY-FOUR

Reflections over Gaza
Michael Yanuck
Waxing Philosophical
Published: Friday, November 23, 2012 11:35 AM CST

Following the joy that my wife and I experienced at President Obama's re-election, the eruption of hostilities in Gaza was a real let down. It left me feeling really depressed; all I imagine are a lot of young people out of work, killing themselves - a lot of death.

Missiles into Israel,
Heading towards a cliff.
Hopeless evil in the world,
Iran's new gift?

Home for the holidays,
All I want is not to hear
Conversations about what's looming,
Unparalleled concerns and fears.

So much for hope,
So much for moving forward.
Just want to take my leave,
Crawl back to my corner.

Brethren, tribe,

I can't help you.
It's too big,
There are too many.

It seems I was mistaken.
I don't want to die.

To be continued.

CHAPTER FORTY-FIVE

Here were my thoughts leading up to last week's poem, 'Reflections over Gaza'
Waxing Philosophical
The Paris Post-Intelligencer, Paris, Tenn., Page 2, January 28th, 2010.

A couple of weeks ago, my wife wanted to dine at a Mediterranean restaurant.

It meant a two-hour ride and we got started later than we wanted. Then, my wife saw a stray dog that appeared lost and trotting dangerously in the direction of the highway, and she insisted that we bring the dog to the veterinarian clinic for safety.

I felt sad that it seemed her act of kindness would mean she wouldn't be able to enjoy the restaurant (it was closing soon), but we drove without stopping and found the restaurant's doors still open as we stepped in.

I was still in hurry mode as I rushed to the counter, so when a big man stopped me and asked about the pre-election button on my shirt, "Our National Healthcare Plan — Don't Get Sick," my response was brief. After the buffet line, my wife and I sat at a table near the wall.

On the wall was a painting that depicted an odd desert scene, with a number of grotesque figures. Coming from a family that had been mostly murdered in the Holocaust, my wife was sensitive to images in the picture as there was the implication of death. But I commented that there were many very beautiful aspects in the painting, too, and just then, the big man who had stopped me before came and sat down with us.

"Let me tell you about that painting," he said. He talked about the picture and then engaged us on a number of different subjects.

He, like my wife, had traveled widely and was even familiar with the tiny strip of beach along the northern Israeli coast where she'd grown up.

Finally, he introduced himself; he was James Abourezk, our country's first Arab-American U.S. senator, who had been among the negotiators at national events like the stand-off at Wounded Knee.

Over the course of several hours, we talked about a range of topics — fighting in Syria, plight of Palestinians and my wife's upbringing in a kibbutz along the Lebanese border. At one point, my wife talked about her cousin, Hanne, a hidden child during the Holocaust and offspring of a doomed marriage between a Jewish opera singer (who died in a concentration camp) and a German officer of the Reich (who went missing at the Battle of Stalingrad).

This turned out to be somewhat of a lengthy discourse, and I was perturbed: Couldn't my wife have just given him a 2-minute synopsis? I wanted to listen to what he had to say.

But Abourezk listened intently, and the following day sent me this email:

"Michael, I had such a good time conversing with you and Sara, I've ordered a copy of my memoir to be sent to you. It's out of print, so this is a used copy, but it reads well in any event. Best regards, Jim."

I wrote him back describing some thoughts from where the conversation had left off; how it is that in my final years, it was my intent to return to Israel and, given my inclination to serve those most in need, I think I'll likely wind up caring for Palestinians in the West Bank and Gaza.

"I am concerned that this path will end in my demise," I wrote, "this a result of tensions in the region, which I'm not ready for yet."

Abourezk wrote back: "Michael, I have a friend who lives in Washington, D.C., who is a psychiatrist. He is a Jew who continuously travels to the West Bank to do what he can to help Palestinians who suffer from trauma. I'll try to connect you with him when he finally shows up out here."

A week later, missiles were being launched from Gaza into Israel. My wife thinks Iran or Syria are likely pulling the strings, either for Assad to divert world attention from atrocities in Syria, or for Iran to step up its enrichment of uranium. The latter matter was discussed during my previous visit with friends and family, and I surprised myself in the extent that I preferred not to think about it.

Now, with plans to return for Thanksgiving, I was dreading a resumption of those discussions, particularly in light of the expanding conflict and potential war in Gaza.

During my travels in Israel 25 years ago, I had been in Gaza. I found it beautiful, with its coast and white buildings and blue skies. I did perceive a tension there, and with the effective boycott of its government over the past years, I can't even imagine what it must be like now?

When I was a boy, I read Elie Wiesel's A Beggar in Jerusalem. A collection of reflections following the Six-Day War, I was moved by its stories of conversations exchanged at the Western Wall, and after arriving in Tel Aviv in 1986, the Wall was the first place to which I traveled.

As a child, I had regarded the Bible as a collection of moral teachings with little basis in fact. But that bus ride to the Wall changed all that; I was walking amidst living history and realized those Bible stories were not fairy tales, but, rather, the chronicles of people of flesh and blood.

I am glad that hostilities in Gaza have been mostly averted. Military intervention would have been horrible for all involved, particularly the region's 2 million inhabitants — men, women and children, for whom I'm sure there are not enough jobs.

> … I thought my destiny lay in Israel,
> Now I'm not so sure.
>
> With so much human suffering,
> I'm inclined to stay afar.

Postscript:

My wife thought that hostilities in Gaza were probably averted because in return for not invading Gaza, Israel was probably "bought off" by the United States, with its willingness to invest more millions into their "Iron Dome" missile defense system.

My father sent me this from Ari Sacher, the primary developer of the Iron Dome: "Without a doubt, Operation Pillar of Defense would have looked very different had Iron Dome not been operational. The system intercepted hundreds of rockets that were headed straight into the heart of residential areas. Iron Dome saved lives, protected property, and gave people a sense of security, something that they had been missing for more than a decade…

"Since 2010, the people of the United States of America have given the State of Israel nearly 300 million dollars for the procurement

of Iron Dome. Another 600 million has been allocated. You people should know that Iron Dome batteries that were funded with American money played a critical part in the conflict. Your money, your help, saved lives."

But will it provide peace? I wonder. All these young people in Gaza – too few with jobs and a future. Without meaningful work, how many of them will chose other forms of expression that involve destruction over creation?

CHAPTER FORTY-SIX

How my family defined our Jewish heritage
Waxing Philosophical
Published: Friday, December 21, 2012 12:21 PM CST

In general, I don't like being in a room where the term "Wachitsu" is used. I feel uncomfortable, especially when I'm the lone non-native. And I find it ironic. As I've stated before, I don't regard myself as white, but rather a member of the Jewish minority.

Shortly before my uncle died, he retold the story of my great-grandfather — where he came from, the life he lived and the religious persecution that brought him to these shores.

"My grandfather, your great-grandfather, was a very religious man," he said. "He would lay stone every morning (a Jewish ceremony for remembering and honoring the deceased). He would go to closing service every night. He would not ride on a Saturday. He would not turn [on] the lights on a Saturday.

"He came from a small town in southeast Russia called Polion; it was part of Ukraine. There were pogroms going on (anti-Jewish rioting in the Russian Empire), and Israel — that was your great-grandfather's name — got to this country in about 1880.

"A friend of his and Grandpa's daughter, Sara, who was about 5 years old, got to this country with him. Her mother had died, and Grandpa took her to America.

"And Grandpa and his friend each acquired a 'knock down' — what would you call it? — a sledge hammer, and he and his friend started knocking down old houses that were vacant and abandoned on the lower east side of New York.

"And they were both very poor. They did not spend their money to rent an apartment, but slept on a workman's bench at night. And they did this for a couple of years for the best I know.

"And back to the point, they would knock down the bricks in the daytime, and after this they would sell the used brick after they had cleaned it up.

"In time, they saved their money and got a horse and wagon and were able to move more brick. They then acquired a small plot of land in Brooklyn, and they had a horse and wagon and let their business grow.

"They ... would take their brick and horse and wagon and move it over to Brooklyn, and then have bigger sales because they were able to haul more brick.

"In a few years, the little piece of property they had in Brooklyn was where the L [train] needed that land, and they acquired quite a bit of money, and Grandpa, as best I know, bought a square mile of land out in Springfield Gardens in Long Island. It had been a potato field.

"Well, the land grew and they started a lumber yard, and then that lumber yard grew, and they started selling coal, and then they started selling oil, and in the meantime, Grandpa had five children, and each of the children came to work in the yard. And we moved to Richmond Hill, and Grandpa picked out the house that each of the children should have, and it was all on one block, and we were a very close family at the time. And so it grew."

There you have it, my Jewish identity as defined by the story of my family — or so I thought.

To be continued...

CHAPTER FORTY-SEVEN

Here *I realized I have German white ancestry*
Waxing Philosophical
Published: Friday, December 28, 2012 11:53 AM CST

A Native American man talked about prejudice in the mostly white towns bordering the reservation.

"Sometimes, you really feel singled out," he said.

I had experienced something of that myself when a white shop owner in a nearby town approached me and said, "I bet you're Jewish ... You know how I know? ... It's your nose! You've got a big Jewish nose!"

I tried to smile at the time, but I found the man's conduct and comment... Well, less than sensitive.

Meanwhile, the Native American man I'd been sharing the story with hadn't as much batted an eye.

"Most of us full-blood Indians have big noses," he said. "That's one of the ways how you can tell who's a full-blood and who isn't."

His comment put me at ease.

"Maybe, it means that I'm a full-blooded Jew," I said.

Later, though, when I raised the matter with my wife of feeling odd when Native Americans regarded me as white, she responded, "You are very light-skinned, Mike. Probably, somewhere in your family, there was is a white European ancestor."

Then, it struck me.

"I knew this," I thought.

My grandmother had told me that she was part-German. She would refer to my grandfather as "Hungarian goulash" (and a "Pollock"), as compared to her superior German stock.

But, until that moment, I could hardly remember a time when I had regarded myself as anything else than Jewish.

"Think of how Hanne must feel," my wife said of her cousin, a hidden child during the Holocaust. "Her father was a German soldier. Her German grandfather nearly turned her over to the Nazis."

How could I have so completely discounted it? I continued thinking. My grandmother was blond with blue eyes. So was my brother.

And being that ones' Jewishness is based on maternal lineage, it could be that my very identity is in question.

In the end, it would take being on an Indian reservation to realize that there was a white part of me — and German, of all things...

Postscript:

Regarding the times my Cheyenne healer-friend, Phillip Whiteman, experienced stereotype and bigotry, he commented, "There were some of those times that were kind of funny. I remember the time I signed up for a rodeo contest. I was at a rodeo, all set to compete. But when it was time to get started, they said that I wasn't signed up.

"They put me in line, and I had to wait for them to check and look for my name in the rooster. They were all giving me all these looks because I was Indian, and there were nothing but a lot of white guys there.

"When I finally got to the front, they still told me they couldn't find me listed anywhere. 'Are you sure you can't find it?' I said. 'The last time I checked, I was the only Whiteman on the list.' She laughed and said, 'I don't think so.'"

As for my grandmother, she had a difficult childhood.

"Her mother died shortly after birth," my mother told me, "and she got put in an orphanage because her father couldn't take care of all those children and work at the same time. There were eight children. She was the youngest."

"Her sister, Sadie, took care of her," my mother continued. "She always looked out for her, and raised her like she was her own daughter. And she never forgot it. She never forgot what she did for her. So when I was a kid, she'd always take me when she'd pick up Aunt Sadie.

"Her dad remarried a woman named Havala. She had a son. She was good to the son, but treated her adoptive children not as good."

Regarding my German ancestry, when I shared my realization with my colleague from Northwestern University, Dr. David Steinhorn, he responded that my German heritage having no place in my identity was a matter of choice; nevertheless, it was in my genes and part of my epigenetics.

"Who knows?" he said. *"Maybe your great grandfather was a great Prussian philosopher?..."*

EPILOGUE

During a hike on Table Mountain in Northern California, my wife and I came upon a burned out and hollow, fallen tree that was still sending branches up from its surviving trunk and reaching to the sky.

"'I am a survivor'," Sara said for it. "If you ever write a book titled, 'I am a survivor', I want you to put a photo of this tree on the cover," she said. "This is the 'Life after the Holocaust' tree..."

I bow my head to this wonderful tree.

Still, so much still confronts us. Indeed, there's the current war in Gaza that I haven't broached in these pages.

If you ask me, more than surviving is the commitment to being righteous

Shalom...

ABOUT THE AUTHOR

Michael Yanuck MD PhD is a physician-scientist
whose groundbreaking research at the National Institutes of
Health was the basis for a FDA-approved vaccine for cancer.
Following a traumatic leg injury he returned to medicine. Intent on
caring for the less fortunate, he enlisted in the National Health
Service Corps, worked in urban and rural health centers throughout
the country, then served native peoples
with the Indian Health Service.

Made in the USA
Coppell, TX
20 May 2024

32612513R00090